Endorsements

Jennifer Morrison's Open Mausoleum Door is an insightful work combining historical inquiry, narrative fiction, and personal memoir. The buildings from the Rush architectural practice are the gateway into the family's personal lives, successes, and loss. It is also a meditation on the connection of subjects to authors, the place of the past in our present day lives, and how this speaks to our own experiences. This is a distinctive and welcome addition to the history of Grand Rapids and the study of local history.

— *Matthew Daley, Grand Valley State University*

Jennifer brings a sense of exploration and adventure to local history. She makes the process of digging into our history come alive. Most of all, she highlights connectedness - pulling threads that run through time, place and people - constantly leading away from and back to each other. Her story is one not just of Grand Rapids history, but of how we are all connected, in ways that we don't always see.

— *Julie Tabberer, Head of Grand Rapids History Center*

I so enjoyed the adventure. It is a book anyone who cares about or is interested in history should read. It is a story of fact and supposition that has been tightly woven together to create a journey worth taking.

— *Gina Bivins, President, Grand Rapids Historical Society*

Open Mausoleum Door

An Entry to the Past is Discovered in Grand Rapids' Oakhill Cemetery

by
Jennifer Morrison

Chapbook Press

Schuler Books
2660 28th Street SE
Grand Rapids, MI 49512
(616) 942-7330
www.schulerbooks.com

Open Mausoleum Door

ISBN 13: 9781957169057

Library of Congress Control Number: 2022904968

Printed in the United States by Chapbook Press.

A Visit to an Old Mausoleum

Bricks and locks and fence protect us from each other.
Flesh and earth and centuries separate us.
You cannot get in.
I cannot come back.

The door between us is dark.
Your only chance of seeing through it is to approach.
Come toward me and press your face against the small pane.

I shall be looking back.

I am not behind a pearly gate or on a cloud or in a palace.
I am positioned squarely in mystery.
And, strangely, here.

Table of Contents

Introduction

I nursed a little research obsession with an architect who lived and worked in Grand Rapids a hundred years before I did, and once when I was looking him up in an old volume of records, I had the realization that I actually knew what he and his family were thinking at a particular point in time. It was a strange feeling. I got a picture in my head of his wife, Delia Rush, in particular, on that day in 1923. It was more than being able to see them across time, though. It was almost like I was with them there, like the day was not fleeting, was not, in fact, long over, was not resolved.

In many ways, this book is a response to that moment of connection.

The strength of it was such a surprise to me that I knew I had to share it with anyone who wished for evidence that our influence can have a tangible effect long after we die. So I started to write about my adventure. This resulted in pieces of memoir about a search that beckoned me into the mysteries surrounding a one hundred year old personal family tragedy. And beyond. Because in order to explore the initial mysteries, I had to pursue broader mysteries about the community surrounding this family and how it changed over time.

The drama and irony of that first moment of connection made the story human and relevant and I knew I had to convey that. I became part of the story, not just as a researcher whose sequential discoveries could reveal the events in the lives of a random group of strangers; but as someone who shared my humanity with a family from an earlier time.

Like many local history lovers who have some of the same infrastructure around them in common with the historical figures we are interested in, I started to imagine how the things recorded in the old documents may have happened. When I converted these pictures in my head to words, it came out as historical fiction.

While I was anxious about whether historical fiction would be viewed as an overly romantic genre for a professional archivist should I ever attempt to publish, I felt relatively comfortable reading between the lines of things like funeral records and census rolls. Maybe too comfortable. It often seemed like I was just extrapolating reality from the sparse truths I did know. But isn't this how we always form an understanding of others, whether living or dead. Ultimately, though, I took the step of assigning action and dialogue and ideas that came from me and not the historical figures in these sections.

There were, of course, times that I could not imagine what the early family endured, and I struggled to flesh out those scenes. In my theory of connection between the living and the dead, I don't know which of us failed at those points.

The story that became important for me to tell was expressed in pieces of writing with different forms (memoir and historical fiction) and from different time periods. It didn't follow chronological order. Eventually I could see that the pieces were arranging themselves like monuments in a landscaped cemetery, seemingly random but together creating a bigger design.

Like an archivist would, I kept careful track of the real documentation. The reader will find that after every chapter of the book is a detailed description of the historical record on which that piece is based. I only pursued photographs after the writing was done, but when I did it made me think about and tell the story in a new way. The reader will also find the photos cited.

Research and writing was the way I acted on my compulsion to honor that sudden and mystical connection I made with a family I never met who were unrelated to me, and bring some resolution to a personal tragedy they suffered over a half century before I was born. The reader may decide if that was accomplished.

June 1, 1923

Grand Rapids Union Station, this building stood on the west side of Ionia at the corner of Oakes Street from 1900 until it was demolished during the construction of the interstate in the late 1950s. It was a replacement for an 1870 building on the same site that became too small for the growing population already thirty years later. Today the area is a parking lot to the southeast of the Van Andel Arena.

Delia Rush was in that painful and awkward position of being forced by social convention to have an experience of profound suffering in public. She told herself that she absolutely must not cry this morning, but while she was tenaciously fighting, she was losing the battle.

She stood on a sloped lane toward the back of a small crowd in a development where all the streets were named for trees. It was 6:20 am on a Friday, the first day of June. The sun had been up for over an hour and it was nearly sixty degrees on a day that would eventually reach eighty. A delicate heel was just visible under her skirt, a boxy hat on her head. She was unconsciously taking small steps backwards, deferring away from the center of activity. She was trying to avoid eye contact and she was getting away with that since Edwin and Jessie were the main focus of attention today.

Delia had returned to Grand Rapids, Michigan, from Tulsa on the Pere Marquette with her husband, Edwin, and his parents, Jessie and Amos. It was nearly fifteen years since they had moved out west.

It was a nice train trip. They bought new clothes for this event. They dressed for meals. The dining car was furnished with white linen tablecloths and good silver.

They left Tulsa on the 29th of May and were three nights on the train, stopping occasionally to switch lines and intersect with Edwin's father, Amos, who traveled separately. The Railway Express Agency made many of the arrangements, smoothing their trip eastward through cities like St. Louis.

But Delia dreaded her arrival in Grand Rapids and the emotional battle she faced there.

In her life, Delia Rush spent a great deal of time as a member of the foursome she traveled with this week. She couldn't remember when she first met Edwin. Though Edwin grew up in little nearby Lowell and Delia was born and raised in the city, their parents were acquainted. Her father, Joseph Randall, was a carpenter. Edwin's father was a stone mason before a long and successful career as an architect.

There was a moment toward the end of high school when Delia was in town shopping with her mother and they stopped by her father's office on some errand, discovering him with Amos and Edwin Rush. The men stood around the large table her father used for meetings, bent over some oversized sheets that were flattened out from a roll. Delia's mother apologized but her father consented to the interruption, as it only required him to walk back to his office with her briefly.

Amos Rush, a man with bright eyes and a bushy mustache curled into points, was dressed in a vest and jacket. He took the opportunity to fetch something from his coat pocket that he'd left in the next room. Edwin had removed his jacket and rolled up his shirt sleeves and when he looked up at her, Delia couldn't tell if he was happy to be left with her or not. They were both eighteen at the time and recognized in the other someone they could potentially find attractive.

Not yet knowing if this was the case, Delia was flippant. The middle child of six, she was naturally assertive, made friends of varying ages and genders easily. "I hope you're working on something interesting and not so dull and old fashioned like the last one," she said, wanting to sound sophisticated after hearing her father relate that a former project presented no special challenges.

Edwin was an only child. He was a young man of some learning, though he was primarily self-taught with little formal education in architecture. His artistic ability was clear in his drawings and a strong asset in his new profession. He was more the serious type, comfortable with solitude, meticulously devoted to his work.

Opposites attract.

Raised to be respectful, he only tightened his lips and looked down at his plans.

"What was the matter with the last one?"

Delia tossed her head slightly, "Well, it had no style! Some of the people in this city think that buildings should all look the same."

"And what type of buildings do you prefer?" He asked without much expression in his voice and without taking his eyes off the table.

"Something more European looking."

"European?" He raised his eyebrows. Had she impressed him or was that disdain?

"Yes, you know. Maybe something that looks like a castle from Europe with some points of interest, like a turret, something with some style." Her ideas were borrowed from her father, but she could not respond well to anything in the way of a challenge in a conversation about architecture.

Edwin crossed his arms and looked at her without reply and just then Amos hurried back into the room.

"Well, Edwin, will we have to make any changes after your conference with Miss Randall?"

Now Delia shifted her attention and it took a second, but when she recognized the gentle flirt, she beamed with pleasure; relief, vindication. Her parents reappeared just then, and as she turned to leave, Delia smiled her appreciation at Amos.

The twist would come a couple weeks later. Joseph Randall returned home for his coffee break with some work one afternoon. As several of the family sat down to apple pie, the elder Randall remembered he had a drawing for Delia to see.

"Me, father?"

"Yes, the building on Monroe has been modified and Mr. Rush told me that Edwin did it on your express directions."

Delia's brother snorted. "Oh, I hardly think Delia knows anything about building design!" He laughed enthusiastically.

Delia's mother shushed him, "Your father is only teasing, John."

"Well, I don't know about that," Joseph replied, "but there's a turret there that wasn't there before and Mr. Rush said Edwin made it for Delia so the building would have some style."

Edwin made love to Delia through his drawings, took her on walks and discussed landmark buildings. It pleased her father when Delia returned from some of these dates and shared things Edwin told her about the business.

The couple were the same age to the year and they had the same first and middle initials. Both Amos William and son, Edwin Arthur Rush, used different variations of their names throughout their lives. Sometimes they went by their first names, sometimes their middle names and sometimes a combination of one of these plus an initial. Delia rarely used her first name but Edwin flirted with her over the coincidence of their initials during their courtship.

Delia and Edwin married on June 6, 1886, in neighboring Greenville. In 1890, the whole Rush family moved to Grand Rapids and Edwin formally joined his father in the architectural firm. The couple lived with his parents. Delia left a bustling home where even the grown children occasionally returned to stay, in exchange for a large house occupied during most of the waking hours only by herself and her new mother-in-law, Jessie.

Jessie, with her red hair and Scottish accent filtered down from her parents, was harder to get to know than Delia expected. Amos and Edwin's business was flourishing. They worked long hours.

The Rush family had been close before the marriage, a perfect triangle with three equal, strong lines, a stable form. Jessie and Amos were proper as any couple from their generation but there was a foundation of gratitude and empathy between them, a vitality in their bond. Amos and Edwin were natural in a relationship that encompassed home and work. Edwin played the role of the beloved son. Undaunted by any personality quirk of his parents that he grew up with, secure in their pride and approval, he pursued his creativity and shared himself with them in their home. He could tell stories, voice opinions or test ideas freely and he would have their attention. He could make his mother laugh. She showed her love to both men as women did then by carefully pressing their shirts, preparing a favorite dish.

It does not occur to men in Edwin's position that a triangle cannot last with more than three points.

Jessie was reserved with Delia. There was some barrier that kept her from a simple show of love toward her daughter-in-law. Delia was awkward in return. She assumed that Jessie didn't like her and it was too easy to conclude that Jessie resented Delia's place in Edwin's affections. Delia couldn't understand that Jessie's motivations were complicated. Delia was too young and self-involved. She hadn't lived long enough to sympathize, not yet.

Delia sought relief from the house and from Jessie by spending more time with friends and her own family, and as a result, caused tension between herself and Edwin.

On the other hand, there was a connection between Delia and her father-in-law that was easy and sweet. Because of their business partnership, Amos had no fear of losing his son to a woman. Instead he gained a pretty, young thing who had not yet heard his stories of professional triumph.

That was the beginning of the four person Rush family. It would come to an end in 1923.

Interior of Union Station. This photo is undated but would be close in time to when the action in this chapter took place.

The Rushes' train pulled in to Union Station in downtown Grand Rapids at 6:04 am on June first, 1923.

Memories of her hometown flooded in on Delia even before she left the station. She began to wrestle with her composure. The slightest thing, a shaft of light on a wooden bench in the waiting area, activated a sharp memory that pricked Delia and drew blood.

She was here before as a young woman, waiting for Edwin to return from out of state. Accompanied by a family member, she went outside for a stroll. When they were alone, he clutched a handful of her hair and staring into her eyes, spoke his special name for her.

It was the specter of this person that tormented Delia on that June morning. It was the loss of a relationship that in many ways meant more to her than any other, a relationship that dramatically and for all time changed the shape of the Rush family.

Delia secretly and briefly found a way to vent her emotions while Edwin was getting the car and Jessie meeting a former housekeeper. She slipped away to the ladies room to weep; indulging her body like it was a small child, in hopes that it would then behave in public. This could never work. There was too much to release, to tap, in a momentary escape.

Failing to manage her grief, she had to rejoin her husband and his parents anyway, the four of them coming together at the baggage express and getting into the car. Delia squinted and drew her lips inward and looked out the window away from the others as if she would find rescue there. Edwin readjusted in the seat next to her and when she glanced at him, he glanced away. Jessie sat on the other side of her, the three of them physically touching but silent.

As they drove south and east, Delia noticed familiar landmarks. It didn't take long for downtown to dissolve into residential blocks as they drove. Quite a few brand new contemporary little bungalows had gone up, filling in space previously more open at this southern point. Delia tried to direct her full attention to such details. They passed South High School, an innovative institution only about eight years old, and then, their general destination came in sight.

They pulled into the park. Soon Delia could see the building, one of the most personally significant that her husband and his father designed. Among those they arranged to meet here was a man they would pay two dollars to bring a heavy decorative key that opened the door.

As they came to a stop, Edwin, protective of his mother, led the older woman out of the car by her elbow. Stepping out after them, Delia's black hem slid up her ankle considerably further than it had the last time she was here. The men took the box from the back of the vehicle.

Despite herself, her eyes lifted toward a spot directly over the door of the mausoleum and Delia confronted the inevitable stone face surrounded by small wings. Tears began to tip over her lower eyelashes and her grief was fueled by her self-reproach.

More than anything, she did not want to upset Edwin or Jessie today.

Ahead of her, she watched Edwin turn back toward her and anticipated his censure. Even then, she tried to withhold. She refused to be the most demonstrative mourner at her father-in-law's funeral.

Berton A. Spring Company

FUNERAL DIRECTORS

Steam Heated Ambulance With Trained,
Careful Attendants

Limousines for All Occasions

EXPERT GARAGE ATTENTION

Jefferson Ave., State and Washington

PHONES: CITIZENS 65056; BELL, MAIN 5056

Ad for the Spring Funeral Home from the 1923 Grand Rapids City Directory. It is unknown why the ad features a white limousine, since they were almost always black, except sometimes for the funeral of a child.

Source Notes

All sources listed throughout the book are from the collection of the Grand Rapids Public Library's local history department, unless otherwise indicated.

This chapter was inspired by the entry for Amos Rush in the Spring Funeral Home records (Coll. #55, Box 8, Vol. 13, entry #83). The information found in this record included a variety of details about such things as the circumstances of the death of Amos Rush, the train trip between Tulsa and Grand Rapids, and the cost of funeral services such as the fee to have the mausoleum door opened.

Details about the weather came from the Grand Rapids Herald from the date of the funeral; the time of the sunrise on the date of the funeral came from the U.S. Naval Observatory website.

Details about train travel came from informal conversations with Carl Bajema, during which I took notes and after which I interpreted his answers to my questions for my story.

In order to describe the trip from the train station to the cemetery, I studied contemporary maps.

General information about the family came from obituaries, city directories; cemetery, census and vital records.

_____

All images in this chapter are courtesy of the Grand Rapids History Center, Grand Rapids Public Library, Grand Rapids, MI.

August 14, 2007 and Related Points in Time

Author photo, taken Aug. 14, 2007.

A voice with a pre-teen edge spoke from the passenger side of the front seat, "I knew it. I knew you were taking me to a grave yard." I turned off the car engine inside the entrance to the south half of Oakhill Cemetery and glanced sheepishly at a red haired twelve-year-old girl sitting helpless beside me.

It's not the same red as mine. Her hair is more coppery and mine is more tomato bisque. Neither of her parents have red hair but then, neither did mine. It's all over in the ancestry, though. It impresses me to have such a tangible connection to relatives I never even met, like the rope on an anchor that appears from under water on the back of your boat. I don't know how to make the metaphor go forward in time, but the trait does.

It was one of the last days of her summer vacation. I told her to wear comfortable shoes but otherwise I had tried to keep our destination a secret.

I'd thought a lot about what this day might mean to her but not much about the implications for me.

Where do I start this story? Several lines of background come together here. I guess I have to tell you about the suffragist and the doughnut and the Christmas gift. And actually, I'm going to have to take you back to the wish I made standing on the eye of the White Horse of Uffington.

I've been a history geek literally as long as I can remember. I had books about the Aztecs and the Incas at the same time I had Barbie dolls. When I was thirteen my mom remarried and my stepdad was in the Air Force. And when I was 16, we were stationed to England for three years. This, of course, was throwing fuel on a quite healthy fire.

Our house was about an hour from it and I probably visited the one hundred plus meter long, prehistoric, white chalk hill figure of a horse at Uffington multiple times. But I specifically remember once standing on the eye of the figure and making a wish, guaranteed according to myth.

When I think of it, it was more like taking an oath. What I said to the horse, or to the universe, or to God, or probably most meaningfully to myself, was something pretty much like, "I'm coming back here in the future and I'm going to have some kind of career preserving history"

As you can imagine, there were a lot of voices around me telling me a career in history wasn't practical, so a tension was building.

Author photo of herself exploring Celtic settlements in Cornwall on holiday in 1977.

As a result, I spent a great deal of time trying to make the pursuit of history for a living into a more practical choice. I never really considered teaching. That field was particularly discouraged and I probably wasn't that interested.

I explored library science briefly in college, and then studied history and literature. These were undeniably my interests despite my ill-fated attempt to tame them with the Dewey decimal system. I knew the job prospects but I was determined, dedicated. I thought of myself as a pioneer.

I earned a BA in public history from Western Michigan University and an MA in public history from Bowling Green State in Ohio.

I did everything I could to get some work experience. All my summer jobs, internships, assistantships and when I couldn't get paying jobs, volunteer work, related to public history. I dipped candles for tourists in a long gingham dress my mom made at my home town's historical village while other kids were making way more money and having much different kinds of adventures during college summers.

Difficult years followed college.

I had a succession of three positions in small, local history institutions with limited resources and major problems. Each time I made a move, I expected the best. Each time I ended up in a quagmire brokenhearted.

Finally I came to Grand Rapids during a divorce. My actual title at the local history department of the Grand Rapids Public Library was "library assistant" and I was half time with few benefits, no health coverage. It was a leap but just exactly the kind of leap "determined" people look back on when they become people who have achieved their dreams.

I had worked a decade at the local history department of the public library part-time and doing other community history work. In lieu of a title like "archivist" or "curator", I started telling people "I do local history stuff." My career was not going to be traditional but things were looking positive for me in the city of Grand Rapids with its vibrant local history community and institutions.

Besides the part-time library gig, there was quite a variety of other jobs I juggled. I did dozens of public presentations, served on boards, wrote for local publications. I developed institutional histories and for several years had a small business with my husband doing personal histories for individuals. One of my sources of extra work was long time City Historian, Gordon Olson, who was my boss at the library when I started there but retired a few years later. Through him I organized the archives of a couple local businesses, helped the YMCA prepare for a big anniversary and completed a series of smaller projects.

One of our more significant collaborations involved writing a book on the history of Grand Rapids' Clark Retirement Community for the organization's centennial. Among the first questions we had to answer was 'who was Clark'?

The book was a good challenge for me and in the process of doing it I basically rediscovered Melvin and Emily Clark, a couple who had a broad impact on Grand Rapids and Michigan but were forgotten over time by most people except their own descendants. The best part was finding all that great stuff about Emily, a patron of the arts, social reformer, and suffragist.

The Clark book had been finished for a year when my husband, John, tempted me into skipping church one summer Sunday morning for something he found more compelling, Marge's Donut Den.

We were thick into the stage where we were trying to get our business to support us and we had no money and no time. Usually there was some huge, labor-intensive task in front of us that would not pay as well as it should, so we didn't do things like pursue leisure on the weekends. But a doughnut-

A doughnut was just the right priced adventure. Marge's was a childhood tradition for John. Then the Grand Rapids Press did a feature on the place and he wanted to go back and take me. I threw on a pair of shorts and a headband and we made the drive across town and stood in a healthy queue. Not a fancy place, it had an air of having missed the last few decades, and glass cases arrayed with about any kind of doughnut you could imagine. My choice had half chocolate and half peanut butter frosting. John took an apple fritter and we split a custard-filled Long John.

We sat at one of the few tables for two near the window and John shared a memory. Once while he was in high school he stopped at Marge's on a double date after a movie. He pulled his 1977 Pontiac Ventura into a parking spot facing the shop, his headlights pointing directly to a couple sitting just inside the window. It was his friend who recognized them. "Isn't that your mom and dad?"

"They would have been sitting right about here," John finished the story.

I asked if he'd acknowledged his parents, or been embarrassed to in that situation. You know teen-agers. It turned out they were all happy to see each other, dates and parents were introduced. I liked that.

I never met John's father. He died of a strain of leukemia diagnosed for less than a week when he was forty-five and John was twenty-one.

This is one of my fascinations with history. The laws of time seem to dictate so much of human experience, including how much access we have to each other, even the people we care about the most; but they don't have the same power over space. I can stand in the very steps, even touch the same physical environment as people who are long gone, or yet to be. I've never been able to resist imagining that there is a connection between people who share the same specific space, even across time.

After my initiation to Marge's, I felt the familiar pressure to return home and get back to work. But getting out, doing something different, something childlike, had an effect.

John asked if there was any place else I wanted to go. "Where could we go for a drive?" he wondered aloud but neither of us could think of an answer. We were unaccustomed to doing things for fun.

"Take Division a little ways." It was the best I could suggest. I liked exploring older neighborhoods, with an escort and a view uncomplicated by having to be the driver. These houses and streets and commercial buildings all made the contradictory claim that once they had been strong and clean. Spaces existing in multiple time periods.

It was on Division that John thought of the ideal excursion, a place I'd been wanting to go for some time but wouldn't by myself. He had the idea to visit Emily Clark.

I knew from work that Oakhill Cemetery was interesting; had some outstanding monuments, held the tombs of some locally prominent historical figures. The genealogists, of course, loved the cemeteries. There was even a period of about three years when I drove past Oakhill regularly to get to the library's temporary location while it was undergoing a major renovation.

My attention then was always focused forward, either on the drive or the destination but I noticed that the cemetery sat in a neighborhood where many of the houses, yards and cars were battered and deteriorated looking and the faces predominantly belonged to people of color. The cemetery had an abandoned feel, as if it were surrounded and cut off by a tide of individuals with completely different needs and perspectives than those buried there.

Within minutes John and I pulled into the south half of Oakhill. John veered slightly off the drive and onto the grass and parked. We weren't sure if this was acceptable but there were no alternative parking options.

The first thing I noticed was a police car sitting still and closed and facing us nearby. We hesitated but set out walking. I thought I knew generally where the Clark monument was and led us to the west. "Supposedly it's over here," I pointed.

Immediately we passed orange fencing surrounding a brick mausoleum that had sections of its walls and roof fallen to the ground around it. The lack of structure and the possibility of what might be exposed had a kind of magnetism that we hurried past to avoid.

The sun was beach day bold and the leaves of the many trees waved just slightly in the breeze. The trees and the little hills made it difficult to see much of a long view. Proceeding down a lane, we quickly grew absorbed by the markers; a stone only the size and shape of a flattened brick that read simply "Father", a lamb reclining atop another stone, a large ornate Celtic style cross.

In such a field of points of interest my eyes struggled to observe each one individually. Promising larger structures in the distance were ignored for what was underfoot and then other times the closest thing was noticed last. There was the feeling of being met by a crowd, all curious, all eager for attention, and some bold about it, making eye contact, even signaling, others demur, hanging back or turning away.

We did not walk far at all before finding ourselves in the shadow of something bizarre. "Are you seeing that too," I asked about half joking as I was dwarfed by a twenty-some-foot tall Egyptian pyramid. It sent an actual thrill down my spine, like vertigo. Standing in the middle of my own city on a peaceful Sunday with no one else in sight and this huge, seemingly ancient, foreign thing in front of me seemed an alteration of reality that might imply others. Like maybe the door would open and we'd be beckoned inside. Maybe we weren't even standing on solid ground.

The door remained firmly shut but in fact, the ground did tend to give way slightly as we left the road and began to wander amidst the head stones. The moles had been at work. We started to pass names we knew, Berkey and Steketee. We circled a grand structure that could have been a chapel or a community mausoleum but there was no view inside. Another was probably a utility building and we wondered what kind of work took place there. We passed a second parked cop car, curious of the significance and doubly concerned that we ourselves looked suspicious.

Not finding the Clarks where I expected, we circled back towards the car and came upon a central diamond shaped section of grass bordered by lanes. It occurred to me that at one time the cemetery may have been beautifully manicured like a park, this diamond more sharply delineated, the bushes neat, the grass green, the urns all filled with flowers. I could picture this a place where people came to walk, possibly even to picnic.

It was on the diamond and near where we actually began our walk that we found a nice little classical shaped mausoleum bearing the name "Clark" and the date "1909". I explained the significance of the date to John. "Melvin died in 1909. Emily lived another twenty years and did a great deal for the community during that time."

By then we were both hooked, though. We wouldn't be getting back in the car for hours.

Adjacent to the Clark mausoleum was an obelisk tall enough that it was impossible to see the top for the tree coverage until we stood directly underneath it, making sudden and unexpected eye contact with the angel on the top. This was the Bissells, Anna and (another) Melvin, the locally well-known carpet sweeper magnates. Melvin died young and Anna kept the company thriving, a rare example of a successful businesswoman for her day.

Behind us was something like a secret garden, an oval shaped section walled off by overgrown shrubs. At one end were stone steps leading to an opening that gave a view of a large tomb marked "Blodgett" at the far end, and here was the lumber baron for whom a hospital was named and his family around him. I had the thought that in life the Bissell, Blodgett and Clark women had been friends as well as associates in social improvement work, and probably the men had also, and the placement of their monuments testified to that.

Continuing over a small hill, we came upon another memorial that could appropriately be called bizarre. A huge rock, Stonehenge proportions, sat elaborately decorated with intricate, ancient looking carvings, with a couple smaller versions near it. We knew the name Kendall from the Grand Rapids school of art. Among the markings on the stone were dates, names and images, the latter of which included a ship crossing a span of waves.

Turning away, we faced a corner of the cemetery that contained only small headstones. Some had fallen and were being overtaken by earth and grass, like water rising, and showed only partial inscriptions. This was the final resting place of those whose lifestyles differed considerably from the Blodgetts and Steketees. Less wealthy and prominent, they would unfortunately be less present in the historical record though equally interesting.

Author photo, taken Aug. 14, 2007.

Having walked throughout the south side of the cemetery, we made a quick
and unanimous decision to do the same on the north side across Hall Street.
There we found just as much to compel us, names we recognized from streets
or businesses or projects, views of stained glass through mausoleum windows,
fabulous forms. As we walked full circle on the north side, our brains and bodies
eventually tired, it was getting hot and late for lunch.

I got in the car and drove away, my mind kind of blown. Back home my imagination was hyper. It shouted ideas for illustrated guides and restoration efforts and children's books. Synapses were firing that hadn't in some time. Grand Rapids was more interesting. Like a heavy ball tossed onto a thin net, the quantum field had expanded. Even my own house felt different that afternoon.

My thoughts returned to the cemetery frequently in the days and weeks that followed. I wondered how the light would be hitting the monuments at dawn or when the sun was warm and soft at the end of a long afternoon, what colors might appear, what shadows would lay where. I thought with some breathlessness about what it would be like to walk the cemetery at night, what sounds if even slight would be sharp to the ear, if the stone would feel cold to the touch. I imagined what would be visible in a heavy snow, where white and gray would trade off, what might loom into view suddenly close.

I had the ironic thought that this cemetery would be an ideal place to bring children. It was essentially an abandoned playground, a Victorian Disneyland. And at some point I associated the experience with the slip of red paper I kept in a basket on my dresser. It was a note from my niece, Caitlin.

My only sibling, a brother, also lived in Grand Rapids. He came to town first and was an important factor in my decision to move here. He and his wife had two children with such vibrantly red hair that it was as if the couple's gene palate was flooded with that single color, as if they could go on creating redheads indefinitely to make up some of the difference between them and other more common hair types.

I had the note since the previous Christmas. It was my present from the oldest niece: a gift certificate to spend the day with her. In order to take advantage of this gift, I would, of course, have to make all the arrangements and do the driving and pay for everything. I loved it. It was an uncommon opportunity and I didn't want to waste it. I'd had the note six months trying to think of the best thing for us to do.

I started to wonder about taking Caitlin to Oakhill. But the two city squad cars we came across that day made me question the safety of the area. I asked a co-worker who lived her whole life in Grand Rapids, "Would you feel comfortable taking your twelve year old niece to Oakhill cemetery by yourself?" "No," was the simple answer. So I considered other things. Family suggested we go to the mall or see a movie or just hang out and do girl things like paint our nails.

Then I asked a second co-worker the same question about Oakhill and got the opposite answer, the one I wanted. Caitlin and I set a date.

Caitlin, probably sensing my angst or getting that message from someone else, called the week before our day and suggested horseback riding. I had to laugh, "I'm not even sure how my body would take that anymore."

"We don't have to," she demurred repeatedly. So I told her to expect an email and sat down to write something I thought would help.

-------------- Original message --------------

From: Jennifer Morrison <Jen@MI-Stories.com>

> Dear Caitlin (and other Interested Parties),

> Here are some thoughts that I've had for our day together. Please review them and let me know of any schedule changes you need to have me make.

> 9:00 am: Retrieval of the girl at her home

> Real soon after that: Convene at a place where you can get like any kind of doughnut you want (my favorite has got half chocolate and half peanut butter frosting but you can choose for yourself)

> As soon as we have our fill: Mystery History Adventure

> (Not all details of the Mystery History Adventure are available in advance as it is something of a surprise. We will go somewhere you have never been before and see rather amazing things that you have never seen before (you've never been to Stonehenge, right? Or to the Pyramids?). This will involve an encounter with important Grand Rapids citizens from the past. (You must be a little bit brave to do this - but I think I'll be okay if you're there with me.)

> Then: Visit the local history department of the Grand Rapids Public Library downtown in order to quench the curiosity we develop during the MHA. Oh, and they have a fabulous young adult section so bring your library card if you have one.

> At Some Point: There must be more treats. We'll have lunch at a hip, downtown destination.

> We can see what else is downtown and there may be some extra time in here when we can consider any other possible cool, fun thing. But then we should visit the market and get just a few things for dinner and you may help with some of the selections.

> 5:30ish: Your family is invited to join us at the Morrison Estate for dinner where we will make a brief slide presentation about the day's events.

> Return Home to sleep, if you're able to after all that (and especially the MHA).

> Substitutions for any activities are allowed at any time before or during the day on Tuesday. You may contact our office with any questions, otherwise we'll see you Tuesday.

Caitlin responded to the email as such:

Hey Aunt Jen, the MHA sounds like a blast. One question, is there anything that would kind of freak me out because you probably wouldn't ever see me again! But everything else sounds nice! Please be honest and tell me if I need to bring any money! Love you so much! See you Tuesday!!!! :)

The stage was set. Caitlin would either hate tramping around a deserted old cemetery or catch some of the excitement I felt about the place. That part was out of my hands. I decided we could abort the plan and head for the mall if things went bad. I picked her up at nine, which gave us time to relax and chat over a doughnut to start. Sipping chocolate milk, Caitlin talked about books and dogs and boys. She would be going to a new school in the fall, starting in a few weeks, and seemed to be handling that well. We finished our drinks and meticulously folded up the tissue that came under the doughnuts and then it was time to do the next thing.

Apparently, from the aforementioned remark, I hadn't kept the secret entirely. I coaxed her out of the car and said, "You lead."

She carried a bag and held it pressed against her stomach with both arms folded over it. We started out in much the same direction as John and I had gone.

She was properly creeped out by the mausoleum that was losing its bricks. Once beyond this, she began to pull me from one thing to another.

So it was that we came upon the pyramid fairly early in our walk and I could fully enjoy her discovery of it. "Stand in the doorway and I'll take your picture," I suggested. Caitlin only shook her head in short, quick, jerks. I laughed and promised that as I'd be looking through the camera lens the whole time, I would certainly warn her if a hand were to reach out for her or something like that.

That was when we were approached. A man moved directly towards us down the lane, stealing my attention and forcing me to think quickly about how to handle a confrontation.

When I'd considered the risks of bringing my little niece here, being alone with her in this neighborhood, I had a vague discomfort with something or someone I couldn't have explained then; but there was one thing I never thought of. During the week, the cemetery was full of maintenance workers. I had to laugh at myself for worrying about feeling unsafe here. This man in a riding lawn mower made a beeline for us but then passed by without stopping. Later John theorized that he may ironically have been nervous of us, as we laughed and snapped pictures, Caitlin ultimately posing on the pyramid stairs.

After this short interruption, it did not take long for me to realize that not only was I having fun, but so was Caitlin. At one point, standing still and looking at a small obelisk surrounded by a short, stone gate, she heard a low mumble and startled only to recognize the buzz of a bee. This thing that seemed like fear was just recognition that there was a presence here that could not be completely comprehended. I felt it both times and it gave this piece of land filled with stones its intrigue and romance and excitement. I was glad to think that Caitlin felt it too.

We made our way throughout the south side of Oakhill coming across many of the things I found interesting on my previous visit. We also saw some things I hadn't noticed before; a stone topped with a three-dimensional carving of a little girl asleep on a cushion and two names underneath, Nellie and Daisy; a stone that looked like it had sunk almost completely into the ground with only the top edge still visible that seemed to have been partially excavated. Near the Kendall monolith Caitlin turned and saw a headstone showing the name "Coffin" and recognized the humor. As we got to that corner, Caitlin claimed to know the term "Potter's field" from some school lesson.

One mausoleum near there had a little bench on the front and I took a picture of her sitting there, wearing a slightly nervous smile, the name "Rush" well over her head. This mausoleum would occupy our afternoon.

The cemetery was only the first half of the Mystery History Adventure. When the schedule seemed to warrant that we move on, I had to coax Caitlin to leave. Throughout our visit, I kept telling her to remember things she was seeing. "If there's anything you notice here that you'd like to know more about, or any of these names stand out, keep them in mind, because this afternoon we're going to see what we can find out about them."

After lunch, we were going to transition from a place I recently discovered to the local history department I knew intimately. I imagined introducing Caitlin to Anna Bissell, about whom there would be abundant documentation, or together seeing what we could discover about the now compelling Kendall. I did, however, want Caitlin to instigate the search, and so I checked myself throughout the morning, determined to let her do that.

Caitlin skipped across the diamond shaped feature on the return to the car and sang over and over, in order to activate her memory, in a silly exaggerated operatic voice, the name "Rush". And this was a family I'd never heard of.

Lunch was at a place with overstuffed chairs and sofas, mismatched candle holders hanging from the ceiling and especially good chocolate chip cookies. The library followed that.

Author photos, taken Aug. 14, 2007.

I have to say I enjoyed walking into my work place in sandals and capris with a child that looked like mine, but no one there had met. A connection was obvious from our hair and I assumed the folks that didn't know better were assuming. There was something fun about this trick. Up in local history of course, my co-workers expected my niece.

I admit pulling the clipping file on Anna Bissell just so Caitlin could see what it was like to find a cache of images and information about a person connected to a monument we just saw.

Then we went after the Rushes. I started with a guess, by pulling a city directory from the 1890s off the shelf and explaining it to Caitlin. "This is almost exactly like a phone book. All the people are listed alphabetically, and then it tells their address, but this also says what they do for a living and where they work. We'll just pick a year and see if there's any, you know, people with the last name Rush."

One name was listed in bold on the page, Rush A W & Son (A Wm and Edwin A), Architects. "Well, that could be them. I think an architect would be prominent enough to have a nice mausoleum in Oakhill cemetery. That's kinda cool, an architect. You know what an architect does, don't you?"

"Maybe. I think so?"

"Well they design buildings. They make drawings of what a new building could look like and then other people build the building. Let's check a few more years of city directories just to see if there's any other possibilities."

As it turned out, A. William and Edwin A. continued to appear in the directories for about a twenty year span and continued to be the only Rush listed in bold. "I'd say there's a Rush that stands out."

I suggested the census next. "Every ten years, the federal government tries to get some information about every single person living in the United States." The census was accessed online rather than in an old, leather bound book and it was fun to show Caitlin both kinds of mediums. I looked over the sources quickly, checking for things that would interest Caitlin, showing her the mechanics of how to search, how to read the findings, explaining how she could even do this from home.

Ruoff Dora, domestic 267 N Ionia.

Ruoff Fred, bds 450 2d.

Ruoff John, carp, h 35 Springfield av.

Ruoff Matthew, blacksmith A Leitelt Iron Wks, h 268 Scribner.

Ruoff Wm, packer, bds 35 Springfield av.

Rupert Arthur E, clk G R & I R R, h 210 S Division.

Rupert Charles A, brakeman L S & M S Ry, bds 185 W Division.

Rupert Charles L, train dispatcher C & W M Ry, h 526 Cass av.

Ruppel Jacob, mach hd G R School Furn Co, bds 157 Scribner.

Rupprecht G Ludwig (Appelt & Rupprecht), h 164 2d.

Rupprecht Joseph J, mach hd Bissell C S Co, bds 164 2d.

Rusch August, finisher, h 194 Davis.

Rusche Joseph P, civil engr G R & I R R, h 38 Waverly pl.

Rusche Mary F, clk H Leonard's Sons & Co, bds 71 S Lafayette.

Rusche Peter J, h 71 S Lafayette.

Rusche Stephen J, shoemkr, 152 E Fulton, bds 38 Waverly pl.

Ruschman Joseph, kettle hd G R Brewing Co, h 627 Jefferson av.

Rusco Charles L, grocer, 93 Fremont, h same.

Rusco Orla B, clk, bds 93 Fremont.

Rusco Pearl G, driver, bds 93 Fremont.

Rush A Wm (A W Rush & Son), h 42 Coit av

Rush A W & Son (A Wm and Edwin A), Architects, 132½ Monroe, Tel 1251.

Rush Charles, lather, bds 150 Kent.

Rush Charles A, matressmkr, rms S East s w cor 5th av.

Rush Edwin A (A W Rush & Son), bds 42 Coit av.

Rush Rev Joel M, h w s Greenwood av 1 n of Michigan av.

Russ George W, sander, h 118 Dayton.

Russ Myrtle, removed to Port Huron, Mich.

Russell Ada R, clk, bds 246 N College av.

Russell Albert B, butcher, h 86 S Division.

Russell Albert B, baker, 138 S Division, h same.

Russell Mrs Anna, h 114 N Pine.

Russell Byron K, inmate Mich Soldiers' Home.

Russell Calvin C, uphol, bds 479 S Ionia.

Russell Charles F, springmkr G R Mattress Co, h 98 Coit av.

Russell Charles H, shoemkr, h 44 Dudley pl.

Russell Charles H, tel opr, h 295 Worden.

Russell Cornelius K, h 354 Fountain.

Russell C Ellsworth, removed to Chicago, Ill.

1895 City directory, courtesy of the Grand Rapids History Center, Grand Rapids Public Library, Grand Rapids, MI.

"Okay, the father's name is Amos William. The son is Edwin Arthur. It looks like Edwin was the only child. Amos was married to Jessie. The son eventually married ... I pointed to the flowery lettering and we both declared it "Delia".

"Then they all lived at the same address. Their office was probably in their house, they worked from home. Okay, and they came from Ohio but lived in Lowell before they moved to Grand Rapids. You know where Lowell is, don't you?"

"No."

"Not too far, you've probably been there. It would be a smaller town than Grand Rapids is."

"Why did they move?"

"Sometimes people move to a bigger city so they can get more business, especially people who work for themselves. Oh, see, and Amos is actually listed as a stone cutter when he lived in Lowell. So he started out working with stone and worked his way into doing something where you actually design whole buildings."

I sensed that Caitlin was following and that she appreciated this. At one point she said, "I like history when it's like this, when you're trying to find something."

We had less luck when we tried for more substantive information on the Rushes in county histories and other sources with biographical entries. We paged through indexes to photographs, since I would have loved to show her what these people looked like but came up empty handed there too.

Our options narrowing and our time running out, I decided to try for an obituary for both men before we had to leave. "An obituary is an article they write about you in the paper when you die. It tells a little story about your life." The local genealogy society members had spent hours creating a good obituary index for most of the twentieth century. It did require some creative thinking as the historical record so far showed a tendency of the Rush men to use an initial in place of a name or a combination of initials and names, but we soon had the relevant pieces in hand.

Grand Rapids Herald, May 31, 1923, p. 3:

> A. W. RUSH, ARCHITECT, TO BE BURIED IN OAK HILL
> The body of A. William Rush, about 70, formerly a
> prominent architect in Grand Rapids, who died at his home
> at Tulsa, Okla., earlier in the week, is expected here Friday,
> and will be placed in the family mausoleum at Oakhill
> cemetery. Mr. Rush, who practiced architecture many
> years, removed to Chicago about 20 years ago and later
> to Tulsa. Becoming established in the latter place, when it
> was only a small city, he took a prominent part in its rapid
> development, designing many structures there. Surviving
> are his widow and one son, E. Arthur Rush.

Grand Rapids Press, October 22, 1948, p. 5

> RUSH – E. Arthur Rush, aged 80 years, formerly of Lowell
> and Grand Rapids, passed away at his home in Tulsa, Okla.,
> Wednesday morning. Surviving are the wife, Delia. Mr.
> Rush will arrive in Grand Rapids early Saturday morning.
> Graveside services will be held Saturday morning at 10:30
> at Oakhill cemetery. Entombment in the family mausoleum.
> Arrangements by Hildreth Funeral Home.

Again, I was hoping for more substance, something that Caitlin might get a kick out of, something she could perceive as relevant. The brief articles did reveal a couple things though. "They're definitely the right people since it mentions the mausoleum."

"And do you see something missing from Edwin's obituary?"

"What?"

"No children. In fact the only survivor listed is his wife, Delia. No one to remember him for one thing and then they moved to Tulsa and lived the rest of their lives there. So no wonder we aren't finding anything much. Who knows what happened to all their family things, their photos, albums, letters, the men's drawings – who knows?"

"They never came back here to live after they moved to Tulsa?"

"No, they died there, see?" I pointed out the relevant text in each obituary.

"Then how come their mausoleum's here?"

"I don't know." I *don't* know.

Ancestors? No, they'd be in Ohio. Why do you get buried where you do? You die there or your family is there. Maybe some kind of good memories in Grand Rapids?

The rest of the afternoon and evening went by quickly. I finished putting dinner together while my brother and John hooked the cameras to the television for a little show and tell that Caitlin and I narrated. Then the girls ate chicken nuggets and curled up under a blanket together on opposite ends of the couch with some new books Caitlin found in the library, while the adults ate in the dining room.

I always enjoy the moments picking up after a dinner party once everyone is gone and recounting it all with John. I was feeling pretty happy about the way the Mystery History Adventure went and excited again with all the potential of Oakhill Cemetery. How fun it had been to have her along and share that with her.

Even the grocery store was fun with her because they happened to be celebrating some big anniversary, so the place was full of people giving away awesome samples, like mini Starbucks frappuccinos. I was shy about it but no one was reluctant to be generous to a cute little red-haired girl.

I set out to interact with my niece by introducing her to some new experiences but she made some introductions herself that day.

I resolved to see if there was anything else I could find out about the Rushes as a treat for Caitlin. For her part, she pretty much forgot about it after that day, like most kids would. Both of us kept and liked the photo of her on the Rush mausoleum bench, the bright sunshine coming from behind me as I snapped the shot, making a windowless and tightly sealed doorway beside her invisible behind a padlocked iron gate; and ironically, neither of us paid much attention to the second face looking back towards the camera from the image.

Source Notes

This chapter relates my actual memories of the day I spent at Oakhill Cemetery and the local history department of the Grand Rapids Public Library with my niece in 2007, as well as events that preceded and followed that day.

I make reference to the following book I wrote with Gordon Olson:

Morrison, Jennifer and Gordon Olson. Caring Community: the History of Clark Retirement Community. (Ann Arbor: Printed and bound by Cushing, Malloy, 2006)

I also reference a mausoleum that was damaged. Eventually. as the following article indicates, it was repaired:

"Historic Preservation Group Volunteers to Restore Mausoleum in Oakhill Cemetery." Grand Rapids Press. July 12, 2010.

Also, the Blodgett plot at Oakhill has now been pruned by members of the Grand Rapids Historical Society into better condition than I found it in 2007.

May 29, 1891

Woman's nightgown originally from the Voigt family now in the collection of the Grand Rapids Public Museum dated "early 20th century".

Delia lay in bed alone. She finished three chapters of a novel hoping Edwin might come, that they might talk or laugh together, might be affectionate. Instead she grew tired of the book and turned out the light and got comfortable on her side, but she couldn't sleep. Normally sleep was a simple matter of breath for Delia. If she could breath deeply, slowly, regularly, that was all it took. But tonight she breathed aloneness; lay in the quiet too alone.

The couple was in their early twenties and married for five years. Delia stopped thinking of herself as a newlywed. Edwin worked incessantly. She saw he and Amos for the evening meal, usually. She had settled into a routine with her mother-in-law.

The Rush home was on Coit Avenue, the second one south of the corner of Coit and Hastings; and the next intersection south was Coit and East Bridge Street, the main commercial center for this north part of town. Most of the merchants at the corner of Coit and East Bridge lived either above or below their stores or quite close by in the neighborhood. Besides two grocers, there was everything from a bakery to an upholsterer there.

The buildings were handsome and tidy. An impressive three-story building housed several of the shops as well as upstairs apartments. The barbershop and the bakery were close enough and similar enough to achieve a fine symmetry to the streetscape. They were both two-story brick buildings with decorative flourishes on cornices and over windows.

Surrounding this hub were residential streets with gravel roads, many trees, and homes of various styles, some quite old. At the west end of Hastings was a unique octagonal house. Scattered to the north and south of Bridge Street were small parks. South of Bridge Street, one approached downtown with its great diversity of architecture, including the St. Mark's Hospital and the new City Hall, the latter designed by Elijah E. Myers, the same architect who did the state capital.

Bridge Street, of course, was also a street with a structure that allowed Delia to cross the river to the west side (where the street was called West Bridge Street) to visit her own mother. There were still children at home there and she visited regularly. The distance was not too far to walk, but especially convenient by streetcar.

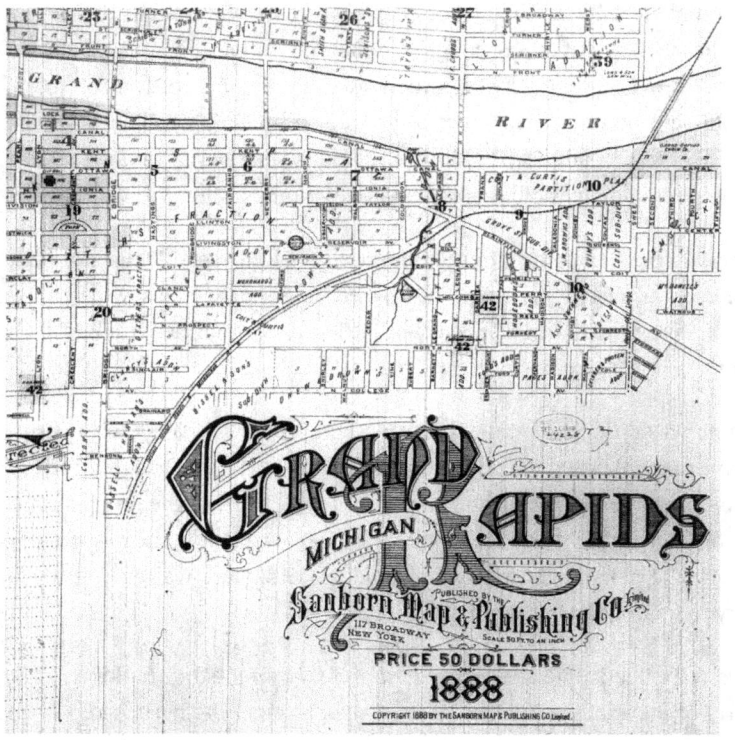

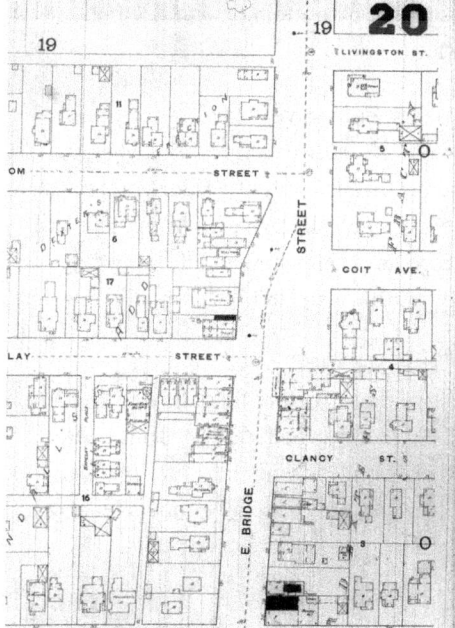

ABOVE: The Sanborn Fire Insurance Company created detailed maps for their own business purposes that are now invaluable resources for the historical research of city streets and structures. This index to the 1888 Sanborn of Grand Rapids shows the area where Coit intersects with Hastings and East Bridge Street. On this map, north is to the right.

LEFT: Detail of the 1888 Sanborn map showing the intersection of Coit with East Bridge Street that was a commercial hub through to the urban-renewal era. North is again to the right on this page of the map.

Having the streetcar at the bottom of the block made downtown similarly convenient to access. The Rush family felt tucked away from the main commotion of the business district while its amenities were still within easy reach. Delia was grateful for her independence.

It was necessary for Delia to coax Edwin to be forthcoming about his work now, whereas that had once been his natural inclination. Things between them could not remain the same as during their courtship.

But his habit of staying in his study alone so late was becoming ingrained and felt vaguely threatening to Delia.

She swung her legs out of bed and onto the floor and got up. Crossing to her vanity, she lit the small lamp next to her mirror, bringing the room back into a stage for activity. She reached for her brush and sat down, but on registering her reflection in the mirror, realized her hair was still perfectly in place.

How she looked was not the problem (after all, even her husband's own father often made remarks about how pretty she was). Getting his attention was. And what to do about that when he was not even in the room? He was downstairs in a cocoon of solitude with his beloved drawings while she had changed into her bed clothes and retired as any decent person requiring a normal night's sleep would.

She turned to face the door behind her, then stood and walked to it. She was positive she heard Amos come up to bed some time ago. Her in-laws' bedroom was just across the landing. Extending her right ear towards the outline of the closed door, she could neither hear nor see anything coming from beyond it. She reached for the door handle but hesitated.

She asked herself then why she balked. Was she worried about disturbing Edwin? Waking the rest of the household? What was this barrier that so effectively kept her in her place and separated from her own husband in their own home? It was all in her mind.

Slowly she turned the handle and opened it a crack. She interrupted only darkness and stillness. Noiselessly, she swung the door open and stepped out into the hall where she could see bright light from the men's study below. In an instant she made the decision to go down.

It was a mild evening and moving on impulse, she did not take the time to put anything on her feet or over her nightgown. This registered with a jolt as she crossed the landing but adrenaline pushed her forwards, not backwards. Her steps were silent.

She descended the stairs, the light from below growing and making her feel increasingly exposed. There was no view into the room without standing in the doorway. The last two steps were before her. She took them and gained the entrance but still could not see anyone. She stepped into the study, turned to the right and then quickly to the left.

No one was there.

Now unsure who was where, Delia was tempted to escape back to her bedroom but she was also intrigued. This was a room that she was normally expected to avoid, in order to let Edwin and Amos accomplish their work. A drawing table stood in front of her.

About half way up it towards the right sat a greasy looking black crayon held there by gravity. She had the urge to pick it up and make some mark but she resisted. Instead she examined a drawing clipped to the top of the board.

The home in the drawing was beautiful and impressive to Delia. She recognized her father-in-law's signature at the bottom left of the sheet and Edwin's a little to the right of that. She also recognized the expressive lines of the artwork that gave the building a personality. To Delia's eye, the house had a dramatic, stylish look. It seemed all roof set upon a heavy, squat base of stone but it had an elegant balance.

The shingled roof did extend steeply down to the first floor but was interrupted by a turret and a gorgeous gable that featured a distinctive triangular shaped window frame over an equally intricate lower story bay. The home's points, its fine carvings, its stonework, and especially the grand carriage entrance with a stone arch that reminded Delia a little of the grotto in John Ball Park, gave it the appearance of a European chateau.

Delia rested her left elbow on a stack of books she did not notice about things like New England residences and the work of Henry Hobson Richardson that sat on a small table near her, and brought her face closer to the drawing. She tried to imagine what sort of room would lie behind the triangular shaped window.

Doing this she was entirely unaware of the man who stepped into the room and approached her from behind.

"Spot a flaw, dear?" Edwin asked.

Delia whirled around and slapped her open palm over her mouth. Edwin stepped back balancing a glass of milk in his left hand and a plate holding an uneven looking sandwich in his right hand.

"You startled me!"

"I see that," Edwin deadpanned and Delia laughed out a little of her excitement.

"What are you doing up?" He set his plate and glass on the stack of books and took a seat on the stool near the drawing table. Delia noticed how his knee rose above his thigh once he sat, how the knee pressed against his trousers.

"Oh, I couldn't sleep. I heard a noise and I didn't know what it was and it worried me and then I wasn't sure where you were -".

Edwin gave her an unconvinced look while taking a bite of his sandwich. Delia sensed he was seeing through her and abruptly turned back to the drawing. "Edwin, whose house is this to be?"

"This will be the new home of Thomas Friant on Cherry Street."

Friant, like many men of the era had gained his wealth from the lumber industry, though his method was a little different than others. While he did buy and sell lumber and lumber mills, he found a special niche that guaranteed him and his partner, Thomas White, a steady flow, as it were, of income. Friant and White ensured that all the other men's logs successfully navigated the Grand River. In providing this service efficiently, they made themselves necessary to so many of the other industry giants.

The business had ceased the previous year, the lumber boom having passed its peak now, but Friant had reached a level of comfort that afforded him this grand home and much more. Lots like Friant's, in the best part of the Hill district sold for a hundred dollars a foot. The house would cost him five thousand dollars.

"Do you like it?" Edwin asked, returning to his sandwich.

"I love it," Delia replied without taking her eyes from the drawing. "Edwin, do you suppose you have any European ancestry? I mean, any aristocratic ancestry?"

Edwin tilted his head and raised his eyebrows.

"Do you ever wonder what kinds of homes our ancestors lived in, if any of them looked anything like the ones you and your father design."

"Hmm, an interesting line of curiosity, E.A., but I think you're being a romantic."

"Maybe you are the romantic yourself, E. A. Weren't these small windows meant for shooting arrows at dragons?" Delia lifted a sheet to show another drawing.

Edwin's eyes laughed a little as he leaned forward to see the feature. "Little dragons perhaps. This is a schoolhouse for Jefferson Avenue. I suppose the principal and the teachers could take refuge in this tower and defend themselves should the students threaten rebellion."

The population of Grand Rapids was growing and there was a recent outcry for more schoolhouses. Grand Rapids was becoming such a large and modern city. The furniture industry in particular was bringing new people in, many of them recent immigrants. Often they still spoke their native tongue and their children were in need of a proper education. Fortunately the field of education had grown quite professional. The board of education was formed twenty years ago to administer all the city schools. Two hundred and forty teachers were currently employed by the board to educate over sixteen thousand students.

Just the previous month the Grand Rapids Eagle quoted the secretary of the board's opinion about the need for more schools, specifically four-room buildings that could easily accommodate additions. Amos and Edwin submitted their plans for an eight-room school for Jefferson Avenue, offering to take two and a half percent of the contract price of the building as their fee and allow the school board to use the plans for more than one building at no additional cost.

In fact as he and his father worked on this project, it often occurred to Edwin that the children would take particular delight in this design. The entrance was underneath a broad stone arch that Amos proposed embellishing with intricate

ABOVE: This April 14, 1894, article from the Grand Rapids Press was one of the main inspirations for this chapter because of the images and descriptions of a variety of Rush buildings.

BELOW: Detail from April 14, 1894, Grand Rapids Press article.

carvings. Over this soared an imposing three-story tower with a narrow corner turret suspended on a corbel. Edwin could imagine little chins aimed upwards in an effort to view the turret's distant pointed roof from as direct a vantage underneath it as possible when they crossed the threshold. These central features as well as others, like the turret shaped dormers that Delia noticed, the stone arch echoed over windows on the front of the tower and on the front cornice would naturally have a fairy tale feel for a child's mind.

That the architecture also impressed adults was a point of more professional pride. The school would accommodate four hundred students who would enjoy the benefits of the latest technology in heating and ventilation. Amos and Edwin had smirked over this last point, sharing memories of the environment in the one-room schools they themselves attended. The two men also did the plans for the addition and remodel on the Wealthy Avenue School, almost as big a project as their new school.

"Show me another," Delia coaxed.

Edwin gave a soft exasperated exhale. "Delia, is this your way of curing your insomnia?"

Delia ignored him and leafed through a stack of sheets, pulling another out. "What is this?"

Edwin finished a gulp of milk, set down his glass and took the drawing from her. He eyed it with a critical frown. "I am fond of this," he added mildly, turning and clipping the page to his board and sitting back down. "It's been commissioned by Mr. Waldron, Lewis, currently involved in the lumber business."

"So Mr. Waldron owns a lumber mill and desires a showpiece downtown for an office. He will then rent some of his extra space to other businessmen for their offices." Delia looked pleased with herself.

Edwin leaned back on his stool and looked impressed. "Quite intelligent, E.A. - and wrong. Mr. Waldron is a bookkeeper – but with ambition." Waldron was the bookkeeper for J.B. White's wholesale lumber, operating out of the Wonderly building, one of Grand Rapids most architecturally significant and centrally located commercial buildings. J.B. White's lumber inspector, Millard Stockwell, and Waldron were negotiating the purchase of the business from White.

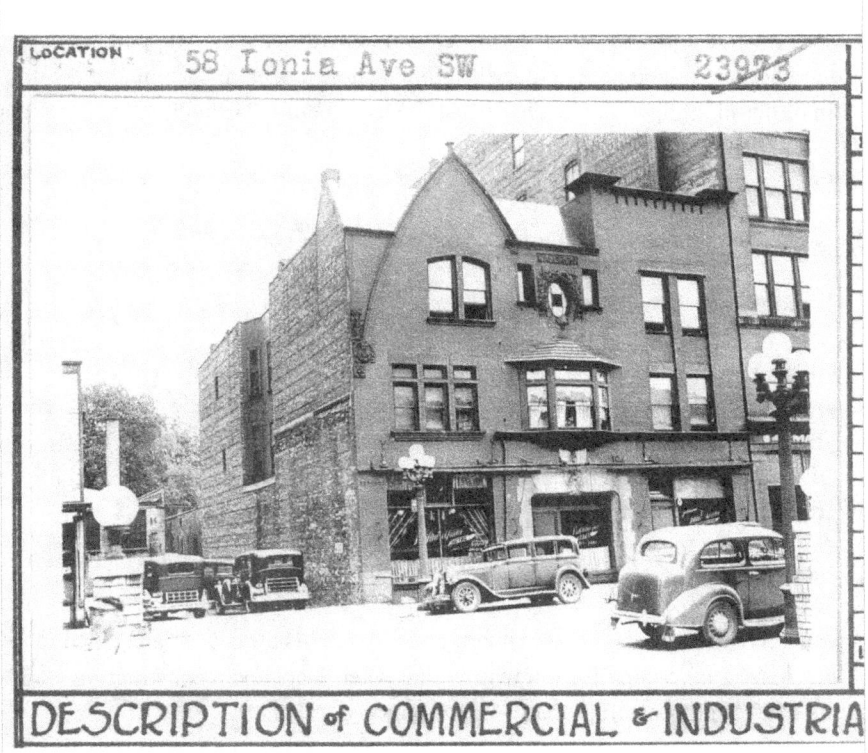

LOCATION 58 Ionia Ave SW 23973

DESCRIPTION of COMMERCIAL & INDUSTRIA

Photo courtesy of the Grand Rapids City Archives

"I can tell you this building will bring him some income. It's going on Ionia, almost directly across the street from Union Station and will operate as a restaurant. The lumber industry may be waning but the furniture they're making from those logs is bringing people in to town more and more and Mr. Waldron will ensure that they don't have very far to look for a place to eat when they arrive."

Delia could see now that the drawing looked like a restaurant or hotel and not an office building. It seemed like the kind of hotel one would see on a fine city street. She could imagine ladies enjoying tea behind one of the picture windows at street level on either side of the front entrance. There was a steep gable, shaped much like the bow of a ship, on the left side of the building as she faced it, balanced by a squared tower shape extending above the roof line on the right side of the building. Between the two was a delicate oval window framed by carvings in the stone, over a second story bay window, above a first floor entrance highlighted by a large flat keystone and voussoirs.

Edwin yawned and was still, then turned and looked at Delia, wrapped his arms around her and pulled her backwards into his chest, his palms gripping the soft satin of her nightgown against her waist. "Are you cold, darling?"

"No."

He sighed and then spoke. "Perhaps your interest isn't casual?"

Delia could not tell what he meant.

"Perhaps you wish to hire an architect yourself, madam? A fashionable new home for yourself, your prominent husband and your several fine children? You seem unsure, let us make a couple drawings." He stood and placed his hands on his hips and looked down at her. "What kinds of features are you especially interested in for your home?"

Delia took Edwin's seat and squinted in thought. "I like bay windows."

"Hmm." He cleared his drawing board and crossed his arms and said, more to it than her, "I am compelled to mention that when it comes to constructing your home a bay window will probably cost a hundred dollars."

"Then I should like three for the front of the house alone."

"Three is an interesting choice, madam," he stared at the blank page. "Anything else?" As soon as he asked, his pencil touched the paper and he began to make some lines.

"Yes, I would like some stone work around the front entrance – an arch I think." He was drawing now and she couldn't tell if it was in any way in response to her.

"Then, again, may I just make clear to you that a carpenter is usually paid two dollars and fifty cents a day. A mason is paid a dollar more."

"No expense is to be spared. My husband and his father are leading architects."

"Is that right? What have they done that I would know? The Taj Mahal by any chance?"

Delia pretended to be in thought. "He hasn't mentioned that. Did I say a shingle roof? I want a shingle roof." It was difficult to see around him or tell what was taking shape yet, but she thought she saw a roofline. She watched his shoulder blades moving against his crisp, white shirt.

"Well, maybe we should discuss some practical issues, like number of bedrooms? What is the size of your family?"

"We have no children yet, but I come from a large family and my husband and I very much agree that we'd like to have a dozen." Edwin interrupted himself only briefly to turn and give her a cross look and Delia smiled to herself.

They both grew quiet, Delia in thought and Edwin in concentration. He drew for a few minutes and then stepped back for Delia to see.

"Edwin!" She looked back and forth from the drawing to him. "It's exactly what I described!"

"Of course."

"But I really like it."

"I like it too," he smiled.

Delia suddenly had a startled look on her face. "Edwin, we could -"

"We could," he mimicked her before she finished her thought.

"But then it would be harder for you to work with Amos."

"Not if we put it on the lot next door."

The look of pure joy that bloomed on Delia's face made him chuckle. He took her face in both of his hands and kissed her.

"And then we could…"

He sighed. "We could. We might get working on that part, actually, if we're going to have a dozen." His hands moved into her hair and he kissed her again better.

Afterward Delia lay in bed again, this time not alone, this time deliberately trying to stay awake. She wanted to enjoy the moment. Edwin had fallen asleep, his arms still around her, making soft breathing noises into her collarbone. The crickets were saturating the night with sound. There was a faint smell of lilac. Delia mentally placed herself in the home that Edwin just drew for her on the adjacent lot to the north of where she lay now. She believed that he made her a house tonight as surely as if he had nailed the last shingle in place. She could tell their children one day about the origins of the structure where they would speak their first words and learn to walk.

As she pictured his house sheltering her while enjoying his physical embrace, there was one more circle within the circle that at that moment existed somewhere between imagination and flesh and bone. Delia herself had just become a shelter. He made a house for her, and in turn she made one for him.

Source Notes

The main inspiration for this chapter was a series of articles in Grand Rapids newspapers describing the work of the Rush architects:

"In Brick and Stone." Grand Rapids Herald. March 6, 1892.

"Our City of Homes." Grand Rapids Herald. April 24, 1892.

"A.W. Rush & Son." Grand Rapids Press. April 14, 1894.

Additional sources of information about Rush buildings included:

Friant home:

"Men of Mark: Thomas Friant, White Pine and Sugar Pine Pioneer." Michigan Tradesman. December 4, 1912.

"Thomas Friant: The Life and Boom Times of a 'Riverman' in Early Grand Rapids." Grand Rapids Press. July 2, 1972.

Personal interview with John Logie, June 11, 2010 now in the Grand Rapids Public Library Oral History Collection (Coll. 164, Box 4, #131).

Heritage Hill Association website, heritagehillweb.org

Jefferson School:

Proceedings of the Board of Education of the City of Grand Rapids 1890-91-92. June 18, 1892.

Twentieth Annual Report of the Board of Education of the City of Grand Rapids Michigan. (Grand Rapids: Dean Printing and Publishing Company, 1892)

"More School Houses." Grand Rapids Eagle. April 14, 1891.

"School Plans." Grand Rapids Democrat. April 3, 1892.

Information on the Waldron Hotel came primarily from city directories.

Details about the neighborhood surrounding the Rush home came from city directories, maps, architectural clipping files and real estate listing cards.

General information about the family came from obituaries, city directories; cemetery, census and vital records.

First image in chapter three is courtesy of the Grand Rapids Public Museum. Image on p. 41 is courtesy of the Grand Rapids City Archives. All others are courtesy of the Grand Rapids History Center, Grand Rapids Public Library, Grand Rapids, MI

After the Day With Caitlin

COMPETITIVE DESIGN FOR SCHOOL—E. *

church this morning, and the occa-   10:30. Evenir
of the bishop

Detail of April 3, 1892 Grand Rapids Herald article showing Edwin's signature.

You can have a pretty intimate relationship with the dead. Standing in Emily Clark's bathroom and admiring her hand painted tile on the afternoon of the Clark Retirement Community centennial book release party the year before Caitlin's and my trip to Oakhill was proof of that.

The party was early in the day at a former home of the Clark's that had since been converted into a restaurant. A few of us hung on afterward, though it was still well before the dinner crowd would arrive, and the restaurant staff offered us our run of the mansion to explore. That's how I came to slip into the master bath and contemplate how slim the separation between she and I was.

Researchers (historians, genealogists, etc.) truly form a relationship with the historical figure. They affect me, they definitely teach me. Some people believe that if the research is going well, it's because the subject is "helping". But I affect them too. I determine whether they "live on". We think so often of the legacy we will leave but much of that is up to those who come after us – to our relationship with them.

And this relationship actually develops a lot like meeting and getting to know a living person. You initiate an acquaintance somehow, maybe someone introduces you, or maybe you get involved in something they were or maybe you just, you know, run into each other in the same space.

At first there's small talk, polite conversation. Then if it goes well, if you show respectful interest, the conversation gets a little more substantive. It's only after the relationship is well established that they share their deepest secrets, the things that are harder to talk about.

Emily Clark initially made herself known as Mrs. Melvin Clark, the wife of this prominent man. Then she seemed to want to be remembered for everything she did for the community. It was like I was being lead from one discovery about that to another. Later, information came about their roots and their life before they were wealthy. I learned that their three children were adopted, which has poignant implications especially considering she helped to found the Blodgett Home for Children. Only toward the end of the project did I learn about their youngest son, the "wild one", who got divorced and who died tragically in his early thirties probably due to the lingering effect of gas after serving in the First World War.

Things would progress in an entirely unique way with the Rushes.

After the day Cailtin and I "met" them, I simply wanted to find a little more to share with her. She and I did all the obvious searches at the public library. I knew that the city cemetery office had some records but wasn't sure if they would contain any information I didn't already have on the family at that point.

So I called. The woman on the phone could tell me who was in the Rush mausoleum and began listing the now familiar names and dates: Amos William Rush, died May 29, 1923; Jessie Crawford Rush, died January 24, 1928; E. Arthur Rush, died October 20, 1948." The most recent to die was Delia who presented her small surprise by being listed in the record as "E. Adelia Rush, died January 17, 1957". I never learned what the E. stood for.

But there were two other details of particular interest to me.

One was that both Amos and Jessie's funerals were arranged by the Spring Funeral Home. That was relevant because the Spring Funeral Home's records were in the collection at GRPL's local history department. I retrieved them for patrons many times.

Now I pulled them again for myself.

Amos, the oldest and first to die of the four family members Caitlin and I discovered, was memorialized in a funeral service at the Oakhill mausoleum on June 1, 1923, three days after his 3:20 am death from "general paralysis" at seventy-eight years of age. His body arrived at Union Station from Tulsa on the 6:05 am Pere Marquette train. The funeral was scheduled for fifteen minutes later. The Rushes paid forty-five dollars for the arrangements, including twenty-five dollars for embalming the body, ten dollars for the hearse from Union Station and two dollars for someone to come and open the mausoleum door.

These details really set a scene. I stood in front of that very door with Caitlin, curious about exactly these people.

I wondered how much clearer a view I could get. One day I asked one of the library's regular volunteers, who had a love of railroad history, what was involved in transporting a corpse from Tulsa, Oklahoma, to Grand Rapids in 1923. Without asking me why I wanted to know, he looked up from his microfilm and gave me quite a description of the system and then went directly back to work.

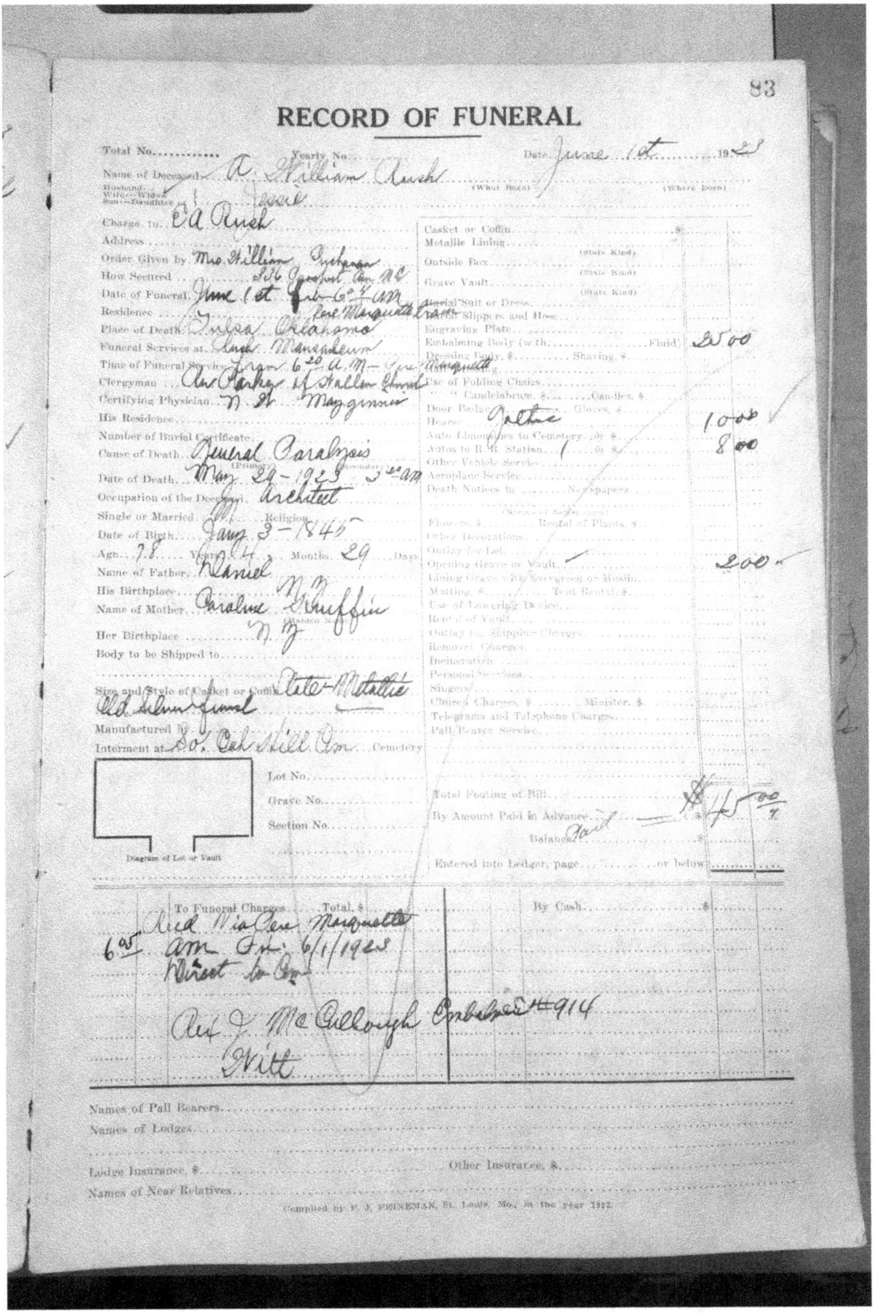

RECORD OF FUNERAL

Total No.............   Yearly No.................   Date _June 1st_ 19_23_

Name of Deceased _A. William Rush_
                                                        (What Street)   (Where Born)
Husband—
Wife—Widow
Son—Daughter _Jesse_

Charge To _O. A. Rush_   Casket or Coffin........ $.........
Address................................   Metallic Lining..........
Order Given by _Mrs. William Buchanan_   (State Kind)
How Secured _S.B. Prospect Ave N.C._   Outside Box............
Date of Funeral _June 1st Jan 6th a.m._   (State Kind)
                                                    Grave Vault............
Residence _Jene Marquette_   (State Kind)
Place of Death _Tulsa, Oklahoma_   Burial Suit or Dress......
Funeral Services at _High Mausoleum_   Slippers and Hose......
Time of Funeral Service _from 6.20 a.m.—_   Engraving Plate........
Clergyman _Rev Parker of Hallen Church_   Embalming Body (with.......Fluid) _35 00_
Certifying Physician _N. H. Magginnis_   Dressing Body, $........ Shaving $....
His Residence......................   Use of Folding Chairs......
Number of Burial Certificate........   " " Candelabrum, $...... Camden, $....
Cause of Death _General Paralysis_   Door Badge...... Gloves, $....
                        (Primary)   (Secondary) Hearse _native_   _10 00_
Date of Death _May 29-1923 3 a.m._   Auto Limousines to Cemetery, $....
Occupation of the Deceased _Architect_   Autos to R.R. Station, _1_....@ $.... _8 00_
Single or Married _M._   Religion........   Other Vehicle Service......
Date of Birth _Jany 3-1845_   Aeroplane Service......
Age _78_ Years _4_ Months _29_ Days   Death Notices in........Newspapers....
Name of Father _Daniel_   Flowers, $...... Rental of Plants, $....
His Birthplace _N.Y._   Other Decorations......
Name of Mother _Caroline Griffin_   Outlay for Lot......
                                                    Opening Grave or Vault..... _✓_   _2 00_
Her Birthplace _N.Y._   Lining Grave...... Evergreen or Muslin....
Body to be Shipped to......   Matting, $...... Tent Rental, $....
                                                    Use of Lowering Device......
Size and Style of Casket or Coffin _State-Metallic_ Outlay for Shipping Charges......
Old Silver Finish   Removal Charges......
Manufactured by......   Incineration......
Interment at _So. Cal Hill Cem._ Cemetery   Personal Services......
                                                    Singers......
                                                    Church Charges, $...... Minister, $....
                                                    Telegrams and Telephone Charges......
                                                    Pall Bearer Service......

        [Diagram of Lot or Vault]   Lot No............
                                                    Grave No............   Total Footing of Bill, $....
                                                    Section No............   By Amount Paid in Advance _Paid_ _$55 00_
                                                                                Balance _Paid_ $....
                                                    Entered into Ledger, page........ or below....

	To Funeral Charges...... Total, $		By Cash.... $
_6.25_	_Died Via Cem Marquette_		
	a.m. Fri 6/1/1923		
	Direct to Cem		
	Act J. McCullough Embalmer H914		
	Witt		

Names of Pall Bearers............
Names of Lodges............

Lodge Insurance, $............   Other Insurance, $............
Names of Near Relatives............
        Compiled by F. J. Feineman, St. Louis, Mo., in the year 1912.

I found a 1927 era map and examined routes between Union Station and Oakhill cemetery, studying the blocks in between and wondering what would have looked different to the Rushes returning to Grand Rapids after fifteen years away. South High School, closed in the present, and the building converted to another function, would have been a new and progressive institution at the time of Amos' funeral, for example.

I came across an ad for the Spring Funeral Home in the 1923 city directory that showed a picture of one of their vehicles. The car was white, a color that I once read was reserved for the funeral of children.

The sun rose at 5:07 am that day according to the U.S. Naval Observatory website. It would have been light for the funeral, the moon still visible. The Grand Rapids Press on that date predicted the temperature would be sixty-one degrees by 7:00 am, building to a high of eighty-three by 3:00 pm.

Having explored as far as I could about a single day in the family's life, my next thought was to see if there might be some information available in Tulsa, where they lived more recently.

I Googled historical organizations in that city. An organization called the Tulsa Foundation for Architecture sounded promising and its website had something. A link labeled simply "Architects" showed a list of names that included "Arthur 'E.A.' Rush". Here was the Rush son going by his middle name with a list of his architectural accomplishments. The first few entries were in Grand Rapids while the rest and the majority were in Tulsa.

The Grand Rapids buildings were Burleson Sanitarium, the Pythian Temple and the Grand Rapids Chair Company. Those in Tulsa included two, the Tulsa Municipal Building, or in parenthesis "Old City Hall", and a bank building, that were on the National Register of Historic Places.

There was also some nice general info about the city. Tulsa experienced a boom initiated by an oil strike just prior to the time Amos and Edwin Rush moved there. This fed an assumption that the men went west in search of better opportunities.

It was nice to find evidence of a career of some substance. I felt kind of proud of the Rushes. I emailed Caitlin a link to the site but her life was filled with things far more relevant to a twelve year old girl. The Rushes quickly became my own obsession.

Post card showing the Grand Rapids Pythian Temple designed by the Rush architects.

Neither the architectural foundation or the Tulsa Historical Museum responded to an email and so after an initial, quick tour of Tulsa, I was back home. I contacted Rebecca Smith-Hoffman, a local historic preservation activist. Rebecca was co-owner of a business that assisted clients with historic preservation issues and was the person the media most often contacted for information on related stories. Almost immediately Rebecca responded with a citation for a newspaper article.

The headline of the April 24, 1892, article read, "Our City of Homes" and it gave a wonderfully detailed description of two houses under construction that were designed by A.W. Rush & Son. I found myself reading about parlors and verandas and butler's pantries and basement vegetable rooms and French pattern porcelain tubs. There was an outline of the plumbing and ventilation systems that I read to John in order to better understand. I started searching Google and Wikipedia for terms like "parquetry" and "electric lighting". It occurred to me then that the Rush men were giving me an education.

Soon Rebecca stopped in to the library with two more articles from Grand Rapids newspapers. One, from 1894, featured drawings and descriptions of over a dozen Rush buildings. The price of construction for them ranged from a two thousand dollar home to an eighty thousand dollar bank building in Sault Ste. Marie. The second article claimed that the Rushes had built $1,351,000 worth of buildings in less than five years.

So they weren't unsuccessful in Grand Rapids, but most likely the move to Tulsa still represented a step up for them.

The drawing at the top of the 1894 article was of a beautiful home labeled "Thomas Friant's Residence". Rebecca spoke of it as if I'd know it. It looked to me like a cross between a British cottage and a castle, with dramatic stonework balancing delicate details. There was a gable with a triangular window and a turret. There was an attachment for a carriage to enter with an impressive stone arch.

I soon realized its relevance. The current owner was John Logie, recent long time mayor of Grand Rapids and also a supporter of historic preservation efforts in the city. This was an exciting connection, one that might even impress Caitlin.

Caitlin and I actually met the mayor for the first time together years before.

It was my first day of work at the library and my brother and sister in law invited me out to lunch at some hip new place on the mall downtown to celebrate. Grand Rapids still seemed big and intimidating which made it ironic to meet the mayor on the first meal out. He happened to be seated with a group of young people a couple tables away from us. On his way out, he stopped spontaneously to flirt with Caitlin. She was two and in the midst of entertaining our table. Her hair, of course, got his attention. Scott introduced us all, pointing out the occasion. Logie declared a shared interest in local history to me, related a few of his accomplishments in that area and welcomed me to my new position.

Over the coming years, I would learn of Logie's central role in the city's historic preservation efforts; but not until I knew the Rushes would I understand how his own home fit into the story.

I stared at the drawing in the article from Rebecca, following all of its lines, and made a discovery. Some of the marks at the bottom of the drawing were letters. I was looking at the signatures of the men in the mausoleum. I wasn't just looking at a drawing of the Friant home, I was looking at *their* drawing. This realization struck me a bit like seeing the handprints associated with prehistoric cave paintings. A signature is a claim at the time it is written, but it is also a direct communication with future viewers, with me.

While hoping for more personal information about the family, the architecture did ultimately capture my imagination. Ironically, the architecture would eventually point back to the family's personal lives.

I was curious about the architecture because of its antiquity, and not just the antiquity of a century as you would expect in our midwestern city. These stone arches, and carved designs and turrets were more ancient. They looked European, something like a castle from Europe. And even more so was the mausoleum, and the other monuments at Oakhill. Fantastical, Da Vinci Code esque explanations occurred.

But the solution to this mystery, the reason for the presence of archaic building forms in Grand Rapids, Michigan, was much more mundane than something Dan Brown would think up.

The work of the Rush men, and that of many others at the time, was simply a response to the whims of fashion.

Trends are cyclical. Often academics can find motivating factors that contribute to these cycles, like economic hardship causing a widespread tendency toward nostalgia.

Our own country's centennial turned our national imagination toward the past. Napoleon's expedition to Egypt that he described for the world in an 1809 book, and a simple persistence of interest in Greek philosophy and culture, played a role in both Egyptian and Greek revival styles being popular near the turn of the nineteenth century.

Rebecca helped me understand this. To her, the Rush buildings looked typical, not exotic like they did for me. She suggested I get a copy of McAlester's Field Guide to American Houses and look up 'shingle style'.

I got the book and two other general works on American architecture and then I kept going. I found two books on mausoleums in the library and started studying cemeteries. Eventually interlibrary loan books and even an adult education class at Michigan State University followed.

I learned as much about cemeteries as I did about more general architecture. I learned there was a distinct shift between the older practice of simple burials and headstones outside a church, accurately known as a graveyard, and the later cemetery proper. It started in Paris in 1804 with the opening of a cemetery called Pere Lachaise.

The rise of modern cities like Paris soon resulted in a proliferation of health problems associated with overcrowding, including amongst the dead. Burial grounds were actually banned in Paris in 1786 leading to the development of the catacomb. Pere Lachaise was designed on a larger, park-like and landscaped property that was originally outside of the city. Its beautiful grounds and elaborate monuments, caught on in the Victorian era of excess.

Such cemeteries eventually swept the United States, often on a smaller scale, like in Grand Rapids. They were called rural cemeteries because of their setting, though by the time I got curious, both Pere Lachaise and Oakhill were swallowed by the growing cities they originally sat outside of, making the name "rural" seem an anomaly.

They were also often called garden or landscaped cemeteries. Tourists flocked to them. Pere Lachaise is still a major attraction. Later they were referred to as Victorian cemeteries.

I was seeing some images of amazing monuments in Victorian cemeteries around the world from miniature cathedrals to full size sculptures of figures to reproductions of ancient structures and I was hooked. The antiquated architecture, the bizarre forms situated on the landscape, strongly compelled me.

In fact I started having dreams of cemeteries, some with fabulous, giant sized architectural features, often in ruins, suggesting an even grander past. In one dream, Caitlin and I explored an ancient cemetery when a storm threatened and we were allowed to shelter in one of the mausoleums.

The thing is, it had been decades since I stood within reach of something so dramatic on the landscape, felt myself caught in its dizzying allure; since I was an excited kid in England poking around true castles and cathedrals and Celtic settlements and vowing to make them my life's work.

At Oakhill, some of that thrill returned.

Appropriately, it put me in mind of early professional landscape artists like Capability Brown that I encountered in England. Working on wealthy estates in the 17th and 18th centuries, these landscapers were inspired by some of the same antiquities as me and sometimes decorated properties with a building or partial building meant to look considerably older, maybe a tower or a 'Roman' wall. These features were called follies. Oakhill, then, was a grand parade of follies.

It made me wonder about the Rushes' own mausoleum where the small bench invited Caitlin to sit, starting all of this. It was actually a pretty little piece of architecture, an Egyptian style stone temple.

There was a figure over the doorway that was interesting, a mid-relief head surrounded by small wings, facing forward. The curious thing is that there was no real face.

I found myself looking into the shape for the familiar mirror image but standing close, slight scoring marks that shaped the oval proved that nothing had worn or broken off. Just a slight indentation that may or may not have been deliberate appeared where the right eye would be. This lack of features was somehow a strong kind of presence itself.

It occurred to me the day Caitlin and I were on the hunt that the Rush men might have designed their own mausoleum. They were architects, Amos was originally a stone mason. But that would have required thinking ahead. Edwin was only a little over forty when the family moved out of the state permanently.

That's another reason I called the cemetery office but I was disappointed to find they had no record of who designed monuments. Many records were lost in a fire that struck their office years ago. If you ever do local history or genealogy, you find out there's often a fire like that to contend with.

While I had no documentation that the Rush men created their own tomb, I would soon make some strong inferences.

I mentioned there were two especially interesting details I learned from the woman in the cemetery office. One sent me to the Spring Funeral Home records and the information there placed me at the scene of a funeral that took place eighty years before Caitlin and I stood on the same site. It was the other detail that put me inside the minds of the people gathered for that event.

This detail, contained in a handful of words, carried the greatest emotional weight of anything I ever read about the Rushes. It was a detail that had power; the power to destroy a family and end dreams, to abruptly halt a legacy. Ironically, it also had the power to resonate through time.

Knowing it gave the funeral of Amos a new dimension.

It revealed that Delia was suffering something more complicated than the loss of her father-in-law. It was an older, more painful wound. It could easily have alienated her from those she was closest to, those with her on the train from Tulsa, just as it had equally afflicted them. It could have been the thing to send them all away from Grand Rapids, to Tulsa, and it definitely brought them back.

The other detail was a fifth name. There were five bodies in the Rush tomb.

In speaking with Rebecca Smith-Hoffman about the Rushes, I gushed about the cemetery in general and Rebecca suggested the two of us walk it together sometime. I found the opportunity just a few months after my visit with Caitlin. We set a date for the last Friday afternoon of October and I watched weather predictions of rain with regret but determination to carry through except in extreme conditions. As it happened, we had a glorious day and ended up spending hours strolling the grounds and sharing what we knew with each other.

Standing beside the Rush mausoleum, we took in its Egyptian revival style, the form classical and yet unique. We noted its red sandstone blocks, the small bench, the featureless face with wings. It was Caitlin who first thought to wonder why the Rush family were here when they finished their lives in Tulsa. And now I knew why the mausoleum was built in Grand Rapids, why the family returned here after moving away to entirely new lives on the other side of the country so many years earlier, Delia nearly fifty of them; why they journeyed from the present to the past; what it meant to be reunited, all five of them.

Long before the family left this city, the first of them was laid to rest in this mausoleum for whom it was almost certainly designed. The first of them was Edwin Rush.

Author photo.

Source Notes

This chapter takes the form of memoir, like chapter two. Since it describes my local history research, sources are detailed in the narrative. Full citations to these sources can be found in the source notes at the end of chapters one through three.

All images courtesy of the Grand Rapids History Center, Grand Rapids Public Library, Grand Rapids, MI.

Halfway. Quite Near My Birthday, Ironically.

The Peter and Gertrude Parbel home formerly at 46 Coit.

The story of Edwin Rush is complicated.

It was a Rush building that helped illuminate this complication for me. This residence had special significance to the Rushes and its history was itself complicated. In fact, it tricked me.

I can be bad with details. They bore me and so I overlook them. This project would ultimately teach me how significant a detail can be, but when I started it, I missed some things. I failed entirely to pick up on a slight variation in a house number on Coit street that was crucial to my understanding of the Rush family.

The home in question was demolished the week I was born. I came into the world far from it and with no connection to it, immediately after the house was erased from the landscape. But half a century later, I developed a fascination with it that led me to seek out one of the members of the family who were living in it at the time it was lost. Her name was Rosemary Parbel.

"Dad used to scold us when we ran across the parquet floor in heels," Rosemary told me over coffee and zucchini bread at her dining room table. I could picture those 40s era women's shoes and some of them had significant heels. Rosemary's father, Peter, cared about that house. He knew what he had there and I loved him for it. The Rushes would be happy.

That was a fun story for me to hear. It was the kind of anecdote I was looking for that day with Caitlin, what I considered more "substantive", something more personal. It was about an entirely different family than the Rushes, but it was a family I could actually talk to about their lives and loves and hopes and dreams and scares and losses, all of which played out in a home designed by Amos and Edwin.

Rosemary's parents, Peter and Gertrude Parbel, bought the house on Coit Avenue well into the Depression. Peter was laid off by the C&O and had to take work doing things like painting and wallpapering. Then Gertie's dad died in 1938 and left her four thousand dollars. Peter thought he might be able to buy a new car. Gertie showed him the house.

They moved in when Louise, the oldest, was nineteen and John, the youngest, was nine. There were six children in all. Peter got his job back at the C&O and had it until retirement. They kept Sally, the 1927 Chevy, and Gertie quietly instructed all six children piled inside to pray when they drove up Michigan hill on their way to the west side for church at St. Mary's. Sally made it every time but they tried to spare her when they could.

Thankfully it was easy for the family to get around without driving. In fact, the house never had a garage or a driveway. The children walked to St. Mary's school. The cross street just south was Michigan, a major thoroughfare since the early days (when it was called East Bridge Street) that featured a commercial hub as well as links to about any other area of the city the Parbels would care to reach.

That corner of Coit and Michigan was the gateway to enough nearby commercial activity to meet the Parbels basic needs for food, household supplies and the children's employment. There was Goudzwaard Hardware and Fairbanks Bakery. Two of the children, Louise and Peter Jr., worked at the Kroger at times. Another, Irene, clerked at the Beedle Brothers dime store that later became Cook's. Peter and Gertrude's account at the Old Kent Bank was the first established at that branch. Gertie would sometimes take a break from feeding and keeping house for her husband and six children to walk down to that corner, sit on the bench and just people watch.

When they moved in, there were still streetcar rails on Michigan and the Parbels themselves came to this corner to catch or be dropped off by the bus. Peter and Louise walked down together one morning early enough that it was still dark. She was waiting for the bus and he a ride to work on the opposite side of the street and until his came, she repeatedly called over to him, "Are you still there?"

The Parbel's house was beautifully made. There was an arched stone front entrance with intricately carved designs above it. There were three bay windows around the door, one on both the first and second floor to the left and one on the first floor to the right. The bay on the right was balanced by a second floor dormer window protruding from a steeply falling roof.

The marble foyer directly inside the entrance was another example of the home's craftsmanship. It served as a small, reliable honor to Peter coming home after a day rebuilding boxcars on Market Street. Walking through his front door had always meant a reunion of some kind for him; with his wife, his children, his kitchen stove that like a dog racing forward at the sound of his master's return, would send some humid smell of good cooking to greet him.

Peter took delight in the home, the oak everywhere, the leaded glass, the solid brass fixtures, the parquet floors. The bathroom had mosaic tile and a tub big enough for the children to stretch out in flat. The library had blue tile around the fireplace and built in bookcases. The beaded built in buffet in the dining room was even featured in the newspaper once when they took Rosemary's sister, Josephine's picture in front of it as she packed for her wedding in Italy where her husband worked briefly for the government.

This image of Josephine Parbel with her wedding dress taken inside the Parbel home before the ceremony was printed in the Grand Rapids Herald on Feb. 29, 1948.

They had a system for sharing bath water among the six children in the early days. Louise and Josephine held a joint graduation party there. John was always coming and going with the various members and instruments of his polka band. There was a chalkboard in the kitchen with everyone's name written on it that helped to keep track of the activity. You crossed off your name with your finger when you came in the house.

They were a lively household there. This struck me as poignant, especially for the irony.

Gertie, who was home the most, set a fast pace all on her own. Not only did she maintain an ambitious schedule of housework beginning with washday on Monday, but she also had an active social life. She was very involved at church. She hosted every kind of party in their home for the children, from birthday celebrations with pin the tail on the donkey to wedding receptions, over the years. She always had a pot of coffee on the stove and almost no one stopped by without sitting for a cup, from the insurance man to the visiting nurse. Gert had several friends right in the neighborhood including a couple of schoolteachers who rented on Coit and women who clerked in nearby shops. During the war, the Navy Mother's Club was like a second family.

Some of the Parbel's strongest memories of the house were from the war years.

For a while there were two blue stars hanging in the front window.

Peter Sr. fought in the Great War, the war to end all wars, the war that was later called by the designation "first". He was both proud of his children and worried for them.

His second child went first which was a surprise. It was hard to see his girl go.

Josephine went out to Washington, D.C., working with men and women from all over the country. She was delighted to become a WAVE, an official member of the United States Navy that was accepting women into support positions due to the international emergency.

It was less than a year after Eleanor Roosevelt helped convince Congress to authorize the WAVES that Jo became determined to join and cheerfully set about accomplishing just that, despite the fact that both Peter and Gert expressed reservations. They couldn't help but at least partly wish she could be happy supporting the war at home like her sisters.

Louise trained for war work at Davis Tech. She took a three-week course that, among other things, sharpened her math skills and her knowledge of the metric system as well as introduced her to a variety of precision tools. She was among the first fourteen women in Grand Rapids to be placed in a factory. The girls surprised their instructors and program organizers with their ability. Louise went to work at the Hayes plant inspecting parachutes and torpedo parts just as she was about to be married.

Louise Parbel appeared on the front page of the Grand Rapids Herald on July 5, 1942, as part of a story on "girls training to be inspectors" at Davis Tech.

Sister Irene attended the U.S. Army's school for weather forecasters newly installed in Grand Rapids and spent her free time mooning over the Dyar boy. More than once Peter had asked after her only to have someone answer, "She's walking John home, Dad."

"But I thought he just walked her home."

"He did, Dad, and now she's returning the favor."

"Well, how long does this go on," he would ask but usually received only sighs and eye rolls as an answer.

Josephine was a different story, though. She was set on joining up and going away. She had inundated them with that song. "WAVES of the Navy," it started out boldly and continued with lyrics about a 'man-sized job' that was done by a Navy WAVE. Finally Peter told her simply, "You be a good girl," and hoped it was enough.

But it was also hard on Peter and Gertrude to watch their oldest son, Peter's namesake, go. Peter junior was truly in harm's way, out in the Pacific helping to conquer the islands. He was battling his way in and building the roads and runways that provided the necessary leverage for the effort. The family talked to Josephine regularly and even saw her, since she was allowed to visit once a year. Peter Jr. was gone for the duration, an expression that meant more than folks even dared admit. At best, it meant gone for an indefinite period of time.

At worst, well.

The family worried and prayed for him.

That period of time was over for the Parbels by the Christmas of 1945.

The war changed so much that was hard to see change. For the Parbels, though, Christmas 1945 was very much about what remained. Rosemary, who would graduate from high school that spring, and John, both still living at home, were there. Louise was there with her new husband. Her last Christmas single, Irene was also there. Soon she and the Dyar boy would have no more need to walk back and forth between houses. Josephine was home from the service. By 1946 both Jo and Rosemary would find work at Michigan Bell, where they were joined by one other sibling, their brother, Peter. Even Peter Jr. was home for Christmas 1945.

When he returned, the family filed into the car and picked Peter Jr. up at Union Station. After they walked in the house from the train station, Peter Sr. strode back to the kitchen refrigerator and offered his son a beer for the first time ever.

Gert made all their favorites that Christmas; chicken and mashed potatoes and sour kraut for dinner as well as homemade sweet rolls, filled cookies and cream puffs, but the joy of the reunion that year, Gertie's happiness, the children's playfulness, tended to wash out the other details.

For Peter and Gert's family, things changed quickly after the war. All was not well in the Midwestern city at midcentury and change was coming. Change had begun a trek through the neighborhood and its main characteristic was persistence.

Six Parbel children, one by one entered careers, married, moved away. The first grandchild was Irene's daughter, Joan, and they didn't stop coming until there were twenty-four. They filled the old house up even more than the children had, using every nook and cranny for their games, including badminton and hide and seek in the attic. Peter retired in fifty-five.

In many ways the rest of the world sped up too. There was so much going on and something new all the time; new construction, new products being marketed. The first televisions sold in Grand Rapids in 1949 and it felt like life hadn't been the same since. Houses went up like crazy after the war, mostly small, single-family bungalows with nearly identical plans. In response, stores opened near the new concentrations and whole new neighborhoods were born. Miles of suburban property were annexed by the city after 1958. Rogers Plaza opened on 28th Street the same year. A collection of brand new stores all essentially under one roof, surrounded by enough free parking for everyone, it was attractive not just to the folks moving down there, but to folks across the city.

Amidst all this new, what was old seemed old fashioned. People used to draw themselves up when they entered Grand Rapids' classical public buildings but by 1962 they were flinging words at them like 'outdated', 'inadequate', 'substandard', 'blighted'. And in the name of progress, they began to be cleared away. There was an urban renewal plan to tear down everything inside a forty-acre patch in the heart of downtown, including Grand Rapids' beautiful old City Hall, the county building, Keith's Theatre.

Some of the implications of urban renewal gained their impetus during WWII. It had something to do with the destruction of the landscape in Europe, the bombs and the tanks shattering old cities, and the rebuilding there. People began to perceive advantages for new development. Eisenhower's admiration of the autobahn ultimately brought another revolution home with that future president. Eisenhower traveled cross-country in the army when he was young and he knew the limitations of America's roads. A transportation system like the German autobahn seemed imperative to the defense of a modern nation.

Eisenhower became President of the United States in 1952, and in 1956, the federal government authorized funding for an interstate highway system. Just a few months later an article appeared on page seventeen of the Grand Rapids Press with the headline, "Expressway May Displace 1,000 Families in City."

That was the north/south route, US131 that was built and opened first. By 1957, the city was beginning to see proposed routes for the east/west interstate, originally called US16. Both highways faced some opposition that caused delays. There were issues with money, as with any major project. The seventeen million dollar price tag for US131 turned into twenty-seven million before it was finished.

It was easy at times for the Parbels to lull themselves into thinking it was all going to miss them. At other times, some development in the process would jolt them into thinking it was coming right for them.

In the end, it didn't take long for it to do the latter. Despite the ups and downs, US131, kept coming. Union Station, where Peter Jr. returned from the war, was flattened after becoming part of the highway's right of way although ultimately not ending up in the path. And the east/west route, now numbered 196, kept coming too. At some point the surveyors started walking through the neighborhood. Then the letter from the right of way agent arrived.

The house did start to seem big after the last of the kids left for good; they took in a renter, Miss Smith, a clerk from a nearby store that Gertie got to know, but it never felt empty. It was full of all variety of things each of them acquired over years; full of layers of whatever remained of all the smells they had generated, full of the touch of their palms on the stair rail, their slippered feet on the kitchen floor, full of echoes of children's laughter.

The letter told Peter and his 68-year-old wife they had to pick all of this up, put it in boxes, and vacate within six months.

The offer for the house that followed was also hard news. The Parbels held out for a while. Then houses started coming down around them, one by one here and there. Sometimes it happened so fast, the families were still moving out when the wreckers arrived. A nearly forty foot deep fissure that dissolved everything in its path advanced toward them from downtown.

People who had been close with neighbors for generations found themselves beside open lots. Pieces of roads were devoured, leaving them unconnected. Routes that had previously led to grocery and hardware stores, work and hospitals were severed, instead now terminating in dead ends. All that was left behind was sand.

At first the sand seemed so innocuous. It was silent, inert. People took pictures of themselves playing in it. One developer told a little boy, "You're lucky because it will be like living across the street from a park."

Then they began to haul in the steel and concrete for the interstate.

Nearly all the houses directly around the Parbels disappeared the fall of 1961 in a symphony of noise and intrusion. It must have been a lonely, surreal winter as the bulldozers began to move east.

Finally they accepted the sixteen thousand dollars, a travesty, and moved into a former rental. The demolition permit for the Parbel's home was signed on Monday, April 9th. I don't know when it actually went down but it was usually within the week. It could have been that Friday, the 13th.

Most of what I know about the house, and especially the family, came from Rosemary. She and I had several phone conversations, and once she invited me to visit. I got to meet her sister, Louise, and see some of the things that the family salvaged when the house came down. We looked at old photos, all black and white, so I wouldn't have known that Rosemary was the only redhead of the family if she hadn't happened to mention it.

She was generous with her memories — from the big picture to the lovely details. Since I was not able to see the house for myself, I asked Rosemary to describe it. It was a grand home. As Rosemary said, "Everything about it was first class." It was what you would expect of the Rush architects. There were rooms that would have originally been for servants. Not counting those, there were just two bedrooms; one with an attached dressing room and one that Rosemary claimed the Parbel family always considered more masculine.

And that's a particularly interesting detail. There was a shadow hanging over the house from very early on, a long shadow that even the Parbels were just able to sense.

Peter Parbel lived another ten years after he lost his home, and in that time the wreckers took many more Grand Rapids landmarks. Despite urban renewal efforts that brought down 128 old buildings, Grand Rapids' downtown suffered a serious decline at the point of Peter's death in 1972. The former hub was marked by closed businesses, abandoned buildings and broken windows.

The same thing happened in the residential neighborhoods. The suburbs flourished and the inner city languished. When I196 was completed, the house across Hastings from the Parbels' and all the houses north of that remained, as did half of the Parbels' then empty lot. The other half of the lot plunged forty feet into four lanes of speeding traffic. Housing values similarly plunged along the route. The interstates came through and the walking neighborhoods disappeared.

The intersection of Coit and Hastings survived the interstate. So did the intersection of Coit and Michigan, directly south of the house. And, in fact, Coit continued to extend north to south as it always did, though today it would require a bridge to traverse over the east/west highway. If the Parbel house had been on the other side of Hastings it would have survived too.

Peter and Gertrude never knew that the home they maintained and loved for over twenty years was designed by Amos and Edwin Rush. In fact, it was designed *for* Edwin. It was Edwin Rush's own home.

When Peter Parbel moved into the house and while he offered up each and every prayer for the deliverance of his namesake from mortal danger during the war, and when he had his first grandchild, Edwin and Delia still actually lived in Tulsa. In fact, Delia died just five years before the home was demolished and then made her final return to Grand Rapids to become the last to be sealed in the mausoleum at Oakhill cemetery.

There she was reunited with the rest of the Rush family in their eternal home.

The area quite near the former Parbel home during the construction of I96. The photo is dated November 1963.

Source Notes

Most of the information about the Parbel family and their years in the home at the corner of Coit and Hastings came from phone calls and my in person interview with Rosemary Parbel Kilmartin, Nov. 24, 2008.

Other information came from city directories, photographs, maps, obituaries, online genealogical resources and the following articles:

"Women Studying War Work to Join 'All-Out' Effort." Grand Rapids Herald. July 5, 1942.

"For a Wedding in Sorrento." Grand Rapids Herald. February 29, 1948.

"Expressway May Displace 1,000 Families in City." Grand Rapids Press. October 25, 1956.

"How Expressway Will Cross North of GR." Grand Rapids Press. March 20, 1960.

"Will Start Buying Land Soon for Int. 96 in City." Grand Rapids Press. January 12, 1961.

"Future Fire Stations, Schools, Parks Eyed." Grand Rapids Press. Dec. 30, 1962.

"Four generations: A family legacy." Davenport University Magazine. Winter 2006.

———————————————————

All images are courtesy of the Grand Rapids History Center, Grand Rapids Public Library, Grand Rapids, MI.

Falls to the Wrecker Unmourned

This post urban renewal aerial view of downtown Grand Rapids, shows I96 extending eastward with Michigan running parallel to the south of it and Hastings running parallel to the north. The homes facing Hastings on the north remained, while the homes that faced Hastings on the south were demolished for the highway.

Fifty years after it was demolished for the interstate, Edwin Rush's home still had something to say. Buildings, it turns out, can speak. They can tell personal secrets.

I was compelled by the fact that the architects in the mausoleum Caitlin and I randomly decided to research created buildings that were so familiar, so visible and accessible to me in my time. But that was not true of all of them, of course. Some were gone. To gain a better picture of why, I had to travel back to mid-century in my research, back to the time the Parbel family was forced to relinquish Edwin Rush's house, back to the time I was born.

I grew up in a fairly small town and was quite naive about what happened to neighborhoods in cities, what made them change, deteriorate, segregate.

I had a vague belief that there was a time in the past when some people did not mix well in close proximity, in homes or schools. I knew the expression, "There goes the neighborhood," mostly a joke insult in my experience, meant something different during my grand-parents' era, the Archie Bunker era. It meant the arrival of Black people.

I didn't know what really went on there, the true connection between "bad neighborhoods" and people of color, and whether the situation was actually in the past. But now at least I developed an objective curiosity. This had more to do with old buildings than social justice but curiosity is a path with a course you don't necessarily control.

Initially compelled by the mystery of why Oakhill Cemetery, a Victorian era showplace filled with pyramids, Greek temples and Celtic crosses, as well as the remains of the city's Progressive era elite, became surrounded by dilapidated cottages, I found myself in the midst of a self-taught crash course on basic twentieth century urban history.

Here's how I started, I went to Wikipedia and looked up 'white flight'.

The 'white flight' entry linked to entries on 'red lining', 'block busting', 'urban decay', 'desegregation' and 'school busing'. A picture began to form in my mind of a diseased evolution arcing off from the first contact between white Europeans and black Africans through to the present; through the institution of slavery and the institution of racism, the development of cities and ultimately to the gates of Oakhill.

I started to see that prejudice against people who were different was not in any way a phenomenon confined to the past. Neither was it simply the response of a few incomprehensible deviants like Archie Bunker, but truly of society as a whole.

Even me.

A memory came to me of the beautiful fall afternoon I walked the cemetery with Rebecca Smith-Hoffman. At one point we proceeded, chatting, up a long, straight section of sidewalk when a single black woman came towards us from the opposite direction. I remember my emotional response, of guardedness. Not because she was black, right? Because we were in a "bad neighborhood", right? As if I thought it was better to be prejudiced against a neighborhood than a person.

I turned towards Rebecca to deepen the conversation as an excuse to avoid eye contact with the stranger. Rebecca, conversely, turned towards the woman as the three of us met on the walk, smiled at her and opened her arms with a remark about the lovely day. The woman smiled shyly and continued past.

The moment, the opposite responses, left an impression on me.

I was following a social contract, I don't even know why, and its terms were this: You and I do not see each other. We occupy the same space but different universes.

This manifestation of my prejudice was a surprise to me, when in reality no one is immune. In fact, in many ways, no one is immune from the damage of prejudice either. Prejudice is not a thing that harms a segment of society, leaving others unaffected. Now I could see that it swept like an invisible flood across the landscape sending people racing from their homes, afterwards leaving things stagnant and spoiled and some things, like Oakhill cemetery and many of the people living around it in the present, marooned. Prejudice tore down things that everyone stood on. It hurt Dutch grandmothers and young black men and old buildings. Not equally, certainly. But I was starting to realize that racial prejudice was not a black and brown issue, but a universal societal illness.

The schools were involved in a way that I did not yet comprehend. Jefferson School designed by Amos and Edwin Rush was located on the south side of the city, not far from Oakhill Cemetery.

The plight of Jefferson School was illuminating for me. With some effort, I found the article that appeared in the Grand Rapids Press when Jefferson was demolished in 1974. The headline read, "Jefferson School Falls to Wrecker Unmourned" and the article continued bleakly,

> "There was no nostalgic community stir, no tears shed, no preservationists to obstruct the bulldozers and crane from swinging into action. Even the Grand Rapids Museum found, "nothing spectacular' to keep, according to Asst. Director Gordon Olson."

A teacher was quoted as saying it was time for the old building to go. The reporter described layers of grime, broken windows, sunken floors and an antiquated heating system.

He also related that,

> "For years, it served strictly middle to upper class white children. But when the boundaries were expanded in the late 1950s, the racial makeup began to change. It served mostly poor black children in its twilight years."

The article speculated whether the "deteriorated inner city neighborhood" could continue to support a school for kindergarten through sixth grade.

The piece did end with Gordon Olson pointing out one thing of value on the building:

> "The only real treasure had to be left behind. 'The front arch represents some good stone carving you don't see on modern buildings, ' he (Olson) explained. 'But it required too much work to remove."

Jefferson School ended its days dismissed even by the historical community but it would not remain 'unmourned' forever. Roughly forty years later I became an exception to that headline.

I knew the maligned heating system was actually a point of pride, as it was state of the art, when the building first opened. The comments from Gordon about the arch were especially poignant for me. It's possible I was the only person alive then who knew the carving on the entrance's grand stone arch was the work of Amos and Edwin Rush.

Undated image of 2nd or 3rd grade class posing at the entrance to what was then called the Jefferson Avenue School. Note the detail on the arch around the front door.

It started to seem like the Rushes taught me about racism and urban development just as they taught me about architecture, that racism and architecture were connected, that a lot of this was connected.

I always hate it when a great old building gets destroyed. It seems like such an unnecessary waste. I think about all the creative forces that brought the structure into existence in the first place and wonder what happens to them. Do they get released to make something new, or are they squashed forever? And what does it mean for the creator, the architect? Does their effort matter anymore? I take it rather personally.

When you invest in a career in history, in many ways you enlist in a losing battle. You dedicate yourself to an element that is perpetually slipping away, whether through demolition or disinterest, and often you feel like the only one who still sees a value.

Then, sure, there are the job prospects.

I continued to work hard combining gigs, part-time jobs and all those things you do for the over-hyped "exposure". Significant advancement seemed the most predictable plot for my life.

I dove in. I signed up for extra hours when they were available. I took on extra projects at the library and on my own time. I got involved with the historical society and the women's history council, serving on the board of each for several years. With much preparation and excitement, John and I launched an entrepreneurial effort revolving around doing personal histories for clients for a fee.

None of it resulted in a promotion at the library, or a different position, nor after John dedicated himself to our business full time, a regular income equal to our expenses.

I held on and plodded on, taking every potential lead seriously and feeling every emotion between panic and surrender along the way. I never entirely gave up hope but it did lose its relevance for me. Whether I could connect to feelings of hope or not, our financial situation was sliding steeply downhill.

Then our archivist resigned unexpectedly after eleven years in the position. I called my mom to tell her and my voice cracked. This meant that I would finally get promoted. All the stars finally aligned: my patience and sacrifice for so many years and my precisely relevant qualifications that put me in the right place at the right time.

But they quietly eliminated the position of archivist at the Grand Rapids Public Library. I never heard a word of protest beyond my own.

Just as creative efforts are vulnerable to obliteration by future generations, there are creative minds incapable of converting their passion into contribution in the first place. Artists, musicians, writers; God or the Universe or whoever's in charge keeps churning them out, but you have to wonder about the point if they can't support themselves or even reach their audience.

I should have been spending all my time on potentially income generating work and a couple of obscure Grand Rapids architects were not that. But I was having fun with the Rush research. In fact, many of the discoveries were a thrill. I was finding so many connections and learning so much. Maybe in the midst of such a long stretch of doing without time or money, it just felt good to do one thing for the pure joy of it.

While engaged in a mundane task at the library, I came across an interesting notation in the finding aid for the Laura Lorenson Photograph Collection. Lorenson was a craftsman, originally from Michigan, whose career took her to both Wedgewood and Spode in England. She returned to Michigan to help the Grand Rapids Public Museum develop a pottery exhibit and ended up staying, retiring in 1954. During her retirement, she made a hobby of photographing what the finding aid described as "some of the architecturally more notable houses in the city." Ultimately her collection was given to the library.

Browsing through a list of descriptions of her photos I came across a line that read "448 Coit Avenue. Built about 1895 by Arthur Rush, an architect."

This was obviously intriguing. I assumed Edwin was going by his middle name and on the day we found them, Caitlin and I learned that the son and father's own house was on Coit.

When we checked the city directories to see how the men's occupation was listed, we saw that they lived together on Goodrich for the first year after coming to the city and then for many years on Coit. Their business was sometimes listed from the same address, other times they had a separate office on Monroe.

I retrieved the Lorenson photo that fit this description and found myself looking at a residence quite reminiscent of Rush buildings. Turning the photo over to look for any other information, I found an index card glued to the back with the description from the finding aid. With one loose edge, I was just able to see under the index card and read slightly different wording on the back of the photo itself, "Coit & Hastings. Originally the Arthur Rush home."

His home. His own home? And designed by him?

I referred back to the city directories the first chance I had. The Rushes first appeared in Grand Rapids city directories in 1890 and on Coit Street, 42 Coit, in 1891. So Lorenson's date was four years too late and the street number was off. To be accurate, all Grand Rapids street addresses changed in 1912. The address would be different in Lorenson's time than when the house was first occupied by the Rush family. There was a source that made the conversion and it also showed a discrepancy. The number was close but different.

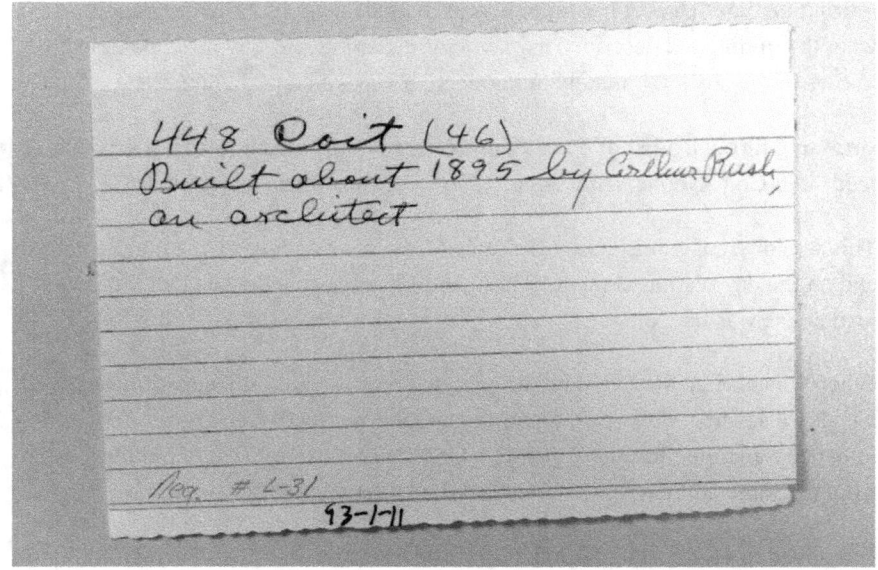

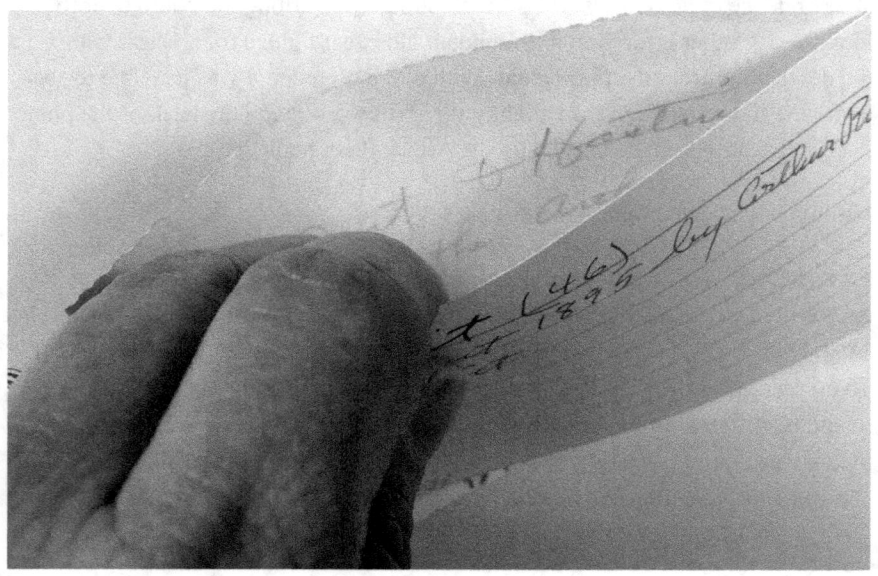

Using the earlier street numbers, city directories indicated the Rush family moved to 42 Coit in 1891 and Lorenson's photo claimed the Rush family moved to 46 Coit in 1895. The two properties were directly next to each other. The house couldn't be in two places at the same time.

At first, I confused myself further by checking a current map. This was not an area of town that I was familiar with and I struggled to get my bearings. I tried to follow the streets and landmarks just north of downtown to the same point where I saw the house, or at least the intersection, on older drawings but the translation didn't seem to work. The area looked different now somehow. Coit and Hastings converged just north of Butterworth Hospital and my brain quickly accepted this as the problem.

A hundred years ago, Butterworth was a large building, but now it was part of a broader system with multiple specialty centers, support operations, parking structures and something under construction all the time. The area was known locally as the Medical Mile or sometimes "Pill Hill" and it changed the landscape quickly and repeatedly over the years.

Trying to figure out how streets and landmarks had changed around the hospital proved to be a distraction though. Only when I stared at the map could I see what was right before my eyes. I was missing the more obvious reason for my disorientation, the thick black extra lines on the current map.

In fact the corner of Coit and Hastings was entirely untouched by hospital development. Both streets extended essentially the same as they had a hundred years earlier. The intersection was unchanged and entirely different at the same time. The area was transformed by those black lines swiping at it from directly south, the lines designating the interstate.

I couldn't imagine Grand Rapids without the interstate. Comparing old and recent maps I struggled to grasp that what was currently a rapid and drastic change in elevation and four lanes of speeding traffic had once been a uniform elevation with regular blocks of quiet streets.

During my research, my step-dad had open-heart surgery at the Meijer Heart Center. One day getting out of a vehicle in the parking structure, I had the realization that we were on Coit Street, just south of the site of the former Rush home. It seemed like two entirely different worlds, the medical mile and the old neighborhood. Coit Street still connected them, though now involving a bridge over the interstate.

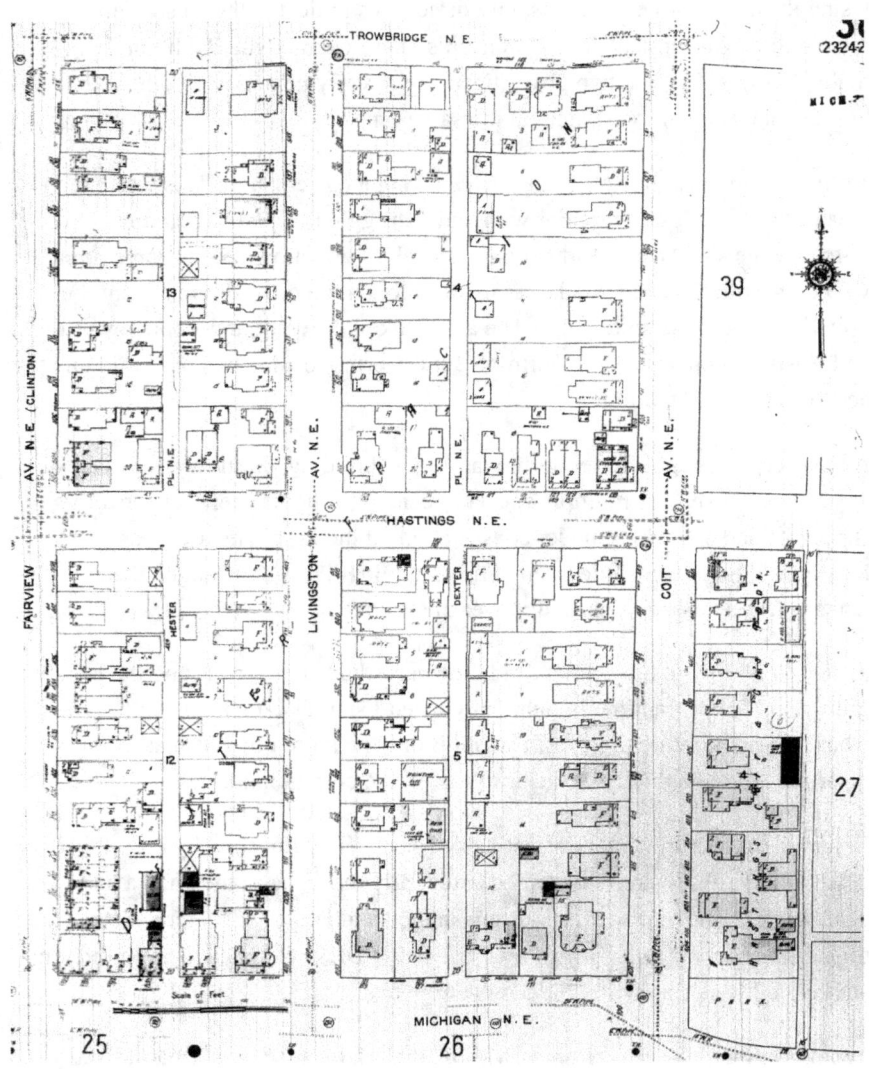

1950 Sanborn Fire Insurance map showing the Parbel home on the southeast corner of Coit and Hastings.

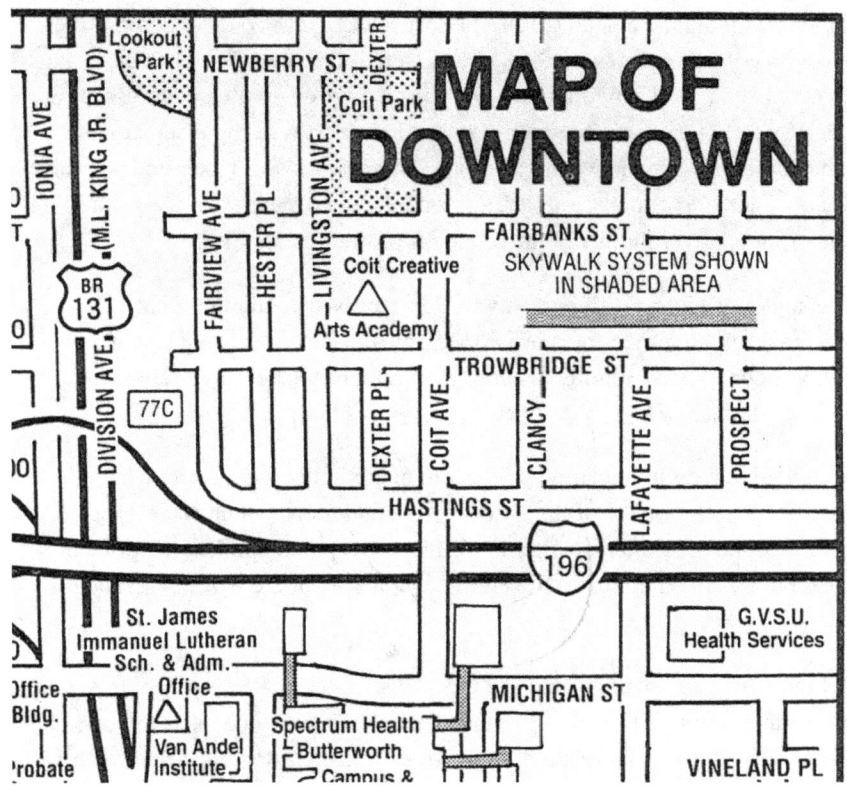

A recent map of the city of Grand Rapids showing the
area around Coit and Hastings today.

I turned my attention to the intersection on the south side of that parking structure, Coit and Michigan (formerly East Bridge Street). I wondered if there was a grocery store somewhere on Michigan that Delia walked to. I found a list of grocers in an 1891 city directory and scanned for one with an address on East Bridge Street. There were fourteen just within a short walking distance, four on the corner of Coit and Michigan alone. There was also a baker and a barber, a druggist and a dry goods, a tailor, a saloon, an upholsterer, and a cigar and tobacco shop, all within two or three blocks of the Rush homes.

It was a glimpse into a different way of life: family-owned individual shops, residences above stores or very nearby, businesses serving specific neighborhoods, grocery stores without parking lots, a level of variety that resembled humanity.

I thought about the implications of this old neighborhood dynamic, what it meant to know the owner of the grocery store and to have them know you, to live near them, to interact with them, and to negotiate, not just the price of things, but to be face to face and negotiate your way in the world with each other.

The highway itself changed much of this. This feature that was meant to aid transportation, to link things, separated so much. So many people used cars and highways to go away. Their attempt was to escape their neighbor, their own past, but both of those things remained attached, straining at the separation, awaiting a confrontation which seemed less painful than the avoidance of it.

Coit Street and its overpass became such a concrete metaphor of the tie to the past that while forgotten, remained. I still remarkably had access to that past and could bring so many of the pieces back together into a nearly complete picture.

It was a meaningful picture. It revealed a great deal about the concept of community.

We went to see the site of the Rush home on a warm April Sunday. I had a vague sense of where it was. I could describe it from a bird's eye view perspective but the highway loomed in my mind as an undefined, consequential interruption.

Approaching from the east, things began to make a great deal more sense in person. I peered at addresses along Hastings and when we thought we were close, John pulled over.

I felt vaguely self-conscious as we got out of the car and locked the doors. There was a pressure from the recessed highway shouting us away and towards a row of parallel houses that did not seem to welcome company.

On the southeast corner of the intersection of Coit and Hastings was a piece of property large enough for a house, at least half a lot, protected by a chain link fence. We stood and stared but could discern no remaining sign of humanity on the precarious piece of grass.

John stepped out onto the bridge over the highway and I followed, but the energy of the traffic below was intense and made me acrophobic. We didn't stay long.

So both addresses were gone now, whatever their connection to the Rush family.

That connection was also right before my eyes. The house wasn't in two places at once. There were two houses directly next to each other that both belonged to the Rushes.

Redundancy does have a tendency to confuse a researcher. Genealogy is harder, for example, when you're dealing with a common name that gets repeated in the same family.

It took reading each and every city directory over again to accept that I was seeing a slight variation in the address of the men's homes over time. It was so slight, it didn't even register with me. Amos, Edwin and their two wives did move in together at 42 Coit in 1891. Then four years later, Edwin designed and built his own home on the lot next door, 46 Coit, the corner lot.

I had to wonder why. It seemed a comfortable arrangement for four adults, two of them working partners. The first home was a larger older home. It couldn't have been an issue of space or privacy for a man and wife in that era. Why go to all the trouble and expense to be directly next door?

Redundancy.

It wasn't just a man and wife that moved into the newer house on the corner. Just as there were two Rush houses on Coit Street, there were, of course, two Edwin Rushes.

Source Notes

This chapter takes the form of memoir, like chapters two and four. Since it describes my local history research, sources are detailed in the narrative.

The following sources were specifically referenced:

"Jefferson School Falls to Wrecker Unmourned." Grand Rapids Press. July 19, 1974.

Photograph, Laura Lorenson Photo Collection (Coll. #93, Box 1, Folder 11)

———————————————————————

All images in this chapter, except those on page 80, are courtesy of the Grand Rapids History Center, Grand Rapids Public Library, Grand Rapids, MI.

September 11, 1898

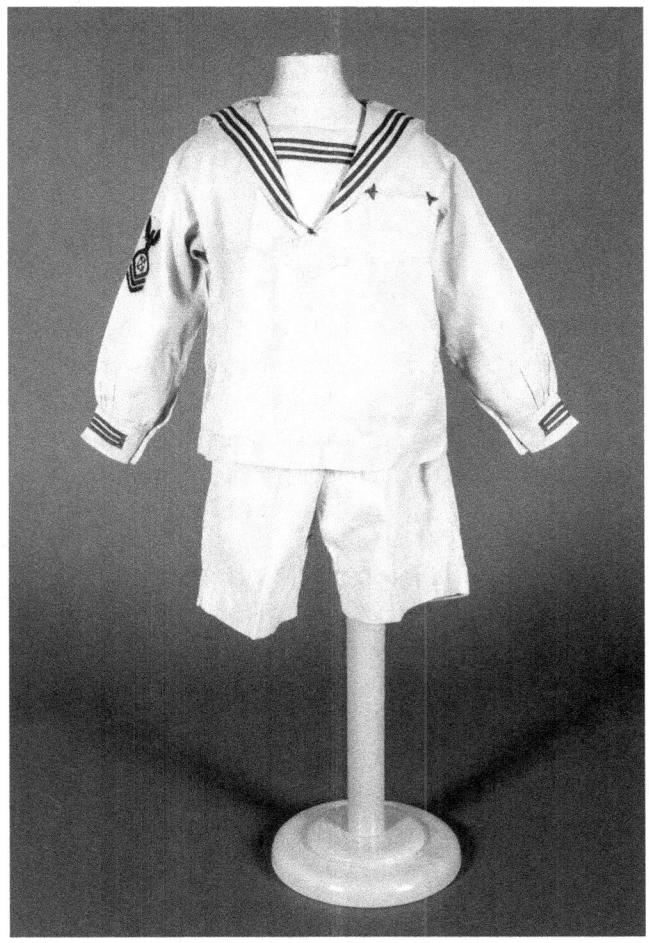

Boy's sailor suit from the collection of the Grand Rapids Public Museum. The estimate of a date for the suit is 1913-1920, although the general style began in England during the reign of Queen Victoria and remained popular for many years.

Edwin was very ill. One glance at the bloody spatter in the bedpan sent snakes of heat racing around Delia's breasts and armpits.

She paced. Not like a man paces, striding back and forth between random stopping points; but like a woman paces, rushing back and forth between things to do, from the damp cloth on his forehead to the bowl of water on the dresser to the cup on the bedside table that she offered but was refused.

Delia's decisions were critical. The relationship that in many ways meant more to her than any other was a terrible weight at the moment. She thought of her own mother who raised six children through all variety of illnesses and made it look like the most natural thing in the world. Then she thought of her mother in law who worried far too much about everything, always jumped to the worst conclusions, and had only one son.

One son.

Just like Delia and Edwin.

On March 14, 1892, Delia and Edwin had a child, a baby boy, and named him after his father. It was six years into their marriage. They were both twenty-four. The first year or two after the wedding, Edwin was relieved. He liked his situation too well, his work, his new wife whose attention he held so completely. But before long, this position of comfort became uncomfortable.

The couple's failure to conceive became the thing that no one talked about, as if acknowledging a problem manifested one. Though this trial did cause Edwin and Delia to develop an unspoken sympathy for each other, a slight protectiveness of the other. They discovered a view beyond the convention of marriage and into each other's humanity. And that, Delia harbored a belief, is what finally ushered the child.

She thought she knew when too, an evening when the year was newly full of the smells and sounds of spring; that season when the impossible is achieved, when life emerges from no life.

With a baby expected, no longer was Delia the house mouse, worrying about whether she was in Jessie's way. She became the center of attention. The other women in her life, her own mother, sisters, girlfriends and cousins, imposed themselves with innocent and happy sociability.

Jessie responded to all of this with quiet determination to be a proper hostess and committed herself to plans for the new addition to the family. She seemed to enjoy the work and this formed a foundation for the relationship between the two women that Delia had formerly reached for but not found, like a swimmer feeling for the unseen bottom of a body of water with outstretched toes.

Occasionally Jessie revealed her nervous nature. Someone would make a remark about the baby's future and Jessie's face would darken or she would mutter a "God willing" but Delia sensed that Jessie was trying to suppress these expressions and forgave her mother-in-law by ignoring them.

Delia had grown to know her mother and father in law well enough by then to see beyond their reserve to the delight her maternity brought them. Delia always sensed a connection between Amos and Jessie, as if they shared a secret, and while it was clear all along that this was a loving connection, it now also seemed a joyful one.

Edwin grew openly pleased. His walk became more like a dance, his speech a little more like the songs men sang in saloons. He became an even more devoted son.

It was seldom now that Delia caught the two architects in the perfunctory silences that attended their long hours of working together. She was more likely to find them elbow to elbow over some drawing, looking up with the smiles already on their faces, having spontaneously convened on something they enjoyed whether or not it was initiated by a client. And often Delia would hear their voices emerge from the office and going in search of them, find them already on their way out the front door, cigars in their teeth and fishing gear in tow, Edwin sending a parting wink her way.

Delia wanted to believe they would all be equally happy with a girl, but there was never a doubt in her mind that if she delivered a son, he would become his father's namesake. Her husband was the beloved only son, the successful architect and partner, and now there was this manifestation of the quality of family for all of them which included (whether the two men had actually spoken of it or whether it spoke loudly enough on its own) a continuation of the multi-generational business.

It was a most delighted reception on the occasion in 1892 that Eddie first projected his voice in the small corner of the world where he found himself.

They marveled at the strength of his voice despite his tiny body. They became familiar with his tiny body, every feature, every aspect. They grew used to his weight in their arms, surprisingly heavy like a dense nut, so much to come forth from it.

He exhausted Delia. She did receive regular help from Jessie who scooped him away and talked to him and rocked him, to Delia's relief. Jessie seemed to have unlimited endurance for him.

Delia had no knowledge whatsoever that on two occasions, Jessie sang Eddie the Highland Fairy lullaby and her face grew dark and she fought tears. The first time, just at the point when she was gripped with emotion, Jessie set the babe down on the floor and walked away from him where she indulged in a brief but earnest fit of sobs before stopping herself and returning to gather him up. The second time she wept and cursed. Her family would have been shocked to see her do either thing. That was the last time Jessie ever sang that specific song.

They watched him grow and develop the muscle to roll over, then to crawl, to stand, to take steps, to race shouting through the house with a hobby horse which caused his father to call him a wild heathen. They listened to his baby babble become toddler logic, laughed when he called the cat a wild heathen.

Late 19th century toy building block set from the collection of the Grand Rapids Public Museum.

Eddie was three when he and his parents moved into the new house. But the planning and building of the structure so close to where they all lived together was a very visible presence in the child's life since almost the beginning. As the work neared completion, the crew would sometimes find Delia holding Eddie by the hand in the doorway of the bedroom that would be his.

They had waited a long time for Eddie and when he made his appearance, it seemed possible that there could be other children. This expectation retreated by the time the home was finished. The house was beautiful. No first class element or detail was spared. It had every modern convenience. It was spacious and it was comfortable. Yet, except for the quarters for the help, there were only two bedrooms.

A single child was certainly capable of filling their lives and each passing year proved that. He was not, in fact, a baby when he died.

He had his first year of school. He was in the beginner's class at East Bridge Street School with twenty-two others his age. The city was growing steadily and the neighborhoods were bursting with children.

The following year he would have progressed to the first grade in a class of over thirty. He was particularly looking forward to his second year of school. They were going to start drawing.

But he got sick right around the time school started.

It began with a complaint of a tummy ache. Delia had trouble getting him to sleep and was forced into the kind of wrestle unique to mothers and naughty children.

He received a scolding from his father but Delia felt sorry for her little boy this time. He seemed so pathetic. Then Eddie woke the next morning with a fever. At first it was almost a relief to have an explanation for yesterday's mood but that was soon replaced by the strain of attending a sick child.

He progressed to vomiting and diarrhea. Delia agonized about whether to have her girl fetch Jessie from next door, or whether Jessie would only make the situation worse. Delia wanted her own confident, competent mother until Jane Randall stood quietly over Eddie's bed with a furrowed brow and Delia discovered the woman's limitations. Eddie lay in his bed in sweat-soaked pajamas, his small features concentrated in pain, his body at the whim of a raging intestine.

After that the doctor was called. He looked serious and said little but examined Eddie thoroughly, putting him through a series of simple tests. There was almost nothing he could do, perhaps administer castor oil, eventually morphine. Delia felt a sinking feeling as the doctor closed his bag and left. She was spent and Eddie seemed worse than ever.

There were sleepless nights. Delia longed for a return to normalcy, to close the door quietly behind her on this thing, to rest with a cup of tea, to return at the end of the day and find it happily resolved. Every minute was an unnatural one, her life confiscated by some inhuman force and held within her view but beyond her touch.

He was pronounced dead at 2:30 on a Sunday afternoon. Delia and Edwin were thirty years old when they lost their only child.

Days.

People. Family. Cups of tea that Delia did not drink and went cold. Visions of Eddie doubled over, or too still from the morphine or death. Food. Getting dressed. A longing for rest. The struggle not to cry at the wrong time, the struggle to cry at the right time. Platitudes, the struggle to seem comforted by them. The longing for solitude, the fear of solitude. A feeling of being carved open by someone with a small paring knife, humming at their work and unhurried.

At the moment of Eddie's death Edwin was outside with Amos, where they stood side by side, each staring into the street, chain smoking and silent. Over time, this circumstance grew in importance for Delia until it felt like an act of betrayal.

But Jessie was at hand almost magically. In memory, Delia was aware of a presence in the room where Eddie lay grotesquely limp. Jessie entered fully into Delia's grief, seeming to understand and offering her if not comfort, then company, some promise of a continued relationship with humanity.

Jessie thought to clip a lock of Eddie's hair for a necklace and Delia never removed this piece of jewelry, often holding it as she wore it. Jessie became a

Mourning dress from the collection of the Grand Rapids Public Museum dated 1894-1896.

lifeline for Delia. She could walk in Delia's world of death and the past while maintaining her place in the present. And Jessie recognized not only Delia's grief but her guilt, offering absolution from the latter before Delia even knew she needed it with such remarks as "You gave that boy everything".

Ironically this did not prevent Delia from developing resentment towards her mother-in-law. Jessie still had the one thing Delia would give anything and everything for, a living son.

But Eddie's death meant that all Delia's relationships became conflicted. Even her relationship with herself, her identity, was conflicted. She saw herself as a woman who was no longer a mother and never would be again. What was she then? A wife?

Edwin seemed suddenly to have a life completely separate from hers.

Her need for her husband was primal and his withdrawal from her seemed similar. She remembered the afternoon; it seemed so soon after Eddie's death, she was in bed, crying and sleeping alternately, attended by women. She asked for Edwin and was told he was working. This shocked her but she was silenced by the presentation of this news as though it were something to celebrate. Perhaps under the weight of such grief, loyalty was possible only to oneself. She should not deny Edwin anything that might relieve a pain this great. It did seem sometimes, though, that men and women alike conspired to protect men from the hardest things in life while women were left to face them.

Edwin returned to his study, his books, his drawing and his natural collaboration with the father who shared his creative inclinations. His first sketches were imaginative; architectural angels, Egyptian temples, buildings the wrong size and shape for any practical use, as if he were indulging his pencil, allowing it to grieve. Amos supported him with full collaboration, the two of them focused soberly on this nonsensical path.

So Delia's feelings towards Amos grew conflicted as well. Amos had always been kind to her, a sweet old man, a gentle flirt that masked a genuine concern, but now he was also supporting Edwin's abandonment.

A new tentative balance framed Delia's world. She had to stand on the small ledge of the good these people represented for her and not fall into the dangers of the bad feelings. Her resentments lapped at her feet, but if she waded in, she would drown.

Before long Edwin and Amos were working with clients again, then traveling. There were projects in process, of course, courthouses in Cass and Grand Traverse counties as well as Rushville, Indiana, among others.

Edwin had a passion, a creative outlet, a reason to live, and Delia was not a partner in it. Men's lives were different. A space grew between them, fueled by avoidance.

But the Rush men struggled with their business about this time.

There was the awful thing with Amos. A woman. Bessie Russell came to Grand Rapids within the first year of mourning. She found Jessie and she made claims on Amos. It was the first the Rush women knew of Bessie and the strangeness of it made her an automatic lie, but Bessie was a difficult and new kind of truth.

Bessie Russell was from the city of Indianapolis, not far from the courthouse project in Rushville. She was twice divorced and she had a fourteen-year-old daughter. Delia was horrified to think that the grandfather of her child could associate with such a woman but it turned out Bessie did know Amos and he was giving her money.

This discovery brought more pain at a time when Delia felt there could be only one source of pain that was more than sufficient to fill a lifetime. Now it seemed fleetingly sometimes as though she was in the process of mourning for just this new loss. Amos told his wife that Bessie was lying and trying to blackmail him. Edwin knew Bessie as well, a fact that opened the door to a cold room at the top of Delia's mind where there were possibilities she hated.

The subject of Bessie came up over tea one afternoon when Delia and Jessie were alone and able to respond naturally. Delia expected anger, disgust from Jessie. Instead Jessie was wistful. "The thing is," Jessie faltered a little which was unusual, "she's about old enough to be his daughter, Bessie."

"Young enough," Delia thought.

"It is as if our fresh loss has unloosed other ghosts." Though she was grave, Delia seldom saw Jessie cry but both women cried then.

Over time the Rush women responded differently to the revelation of Bessie

Russell. Ironically Jessie sympathized with her husband and Delia thought she sensed a new tenderness between them as they entered old age. Delia, on the other hand, could not so easily find her way to forgiveness, not just of Amos, but of Edwin.

Difficult years followed.

Edwin's dream of producing an architectural journal was beginning to come true about the time of Eddie's death. The men took a partner in Grand Rapids towards this objective, named William Bowman, who moved into Amos and Jessie's home. They named the journal the American Modern Builder. Amos and Bowman fought, however, about the direction of the business and about money. As a new century bloomed, Bowman sued the Rushes and Edwin never attempted a journal again.

Park
or Wright-

School
ælph h 13

ne
8 Barry av
'9 W Ran-

Ruprecht)

Oakdale av
9 W Ran

Rhodes av

on

arles Lynn

Winona
eld av

Peter (Rusetos Bros) 470 W Chicago av h 323 N Ashland av
Rush Albert L clk 208 Monroe h 5556 Drexel av
Andrew lab h rear 959 W Vanburen
Andrew saloon 160 W Jackson boul h 529 W 12th
Anna T wid Harold h 32 Wendell
A William (A W Rush & Co) 410, 188 Madison h 3650 Wabash av
RUSH A W & CO (A William Rush) architects 410, 188 Madison
Bartley engineer h 213, 80th
Blanche E Miss h 3853 Langley av
B agt 555 W 63d h 410 W 61st
Charles cook bds 1306 Wabash av
Charles oiler bds 210, 92d
Charles tanner h 193 Mohawk
RUSH CITY EXPRESS I S Coles prop 71 E Harrison tel Harrison-2632
David G sec Masonic Fraternity Temple assn 1019 Masonic Temple h 519 W Adams
Edward J h 97 Kendall
Edwin A clk 410, 188 Madison h 3650 Wabash av
Edwin F physician h 173 Winthrop av
Elizabeth Miss clk h 54 Cypress
Emma Miss h 243 Ogden av
Frank brewer h 241, 24th pl
Frank G clk Great Northern hotel
Fred lab h 79 W 24th
George lab h 122 W Huron
Gustav clk State ne cor Washington h 269 Huron
RUSH G FRED (Rush & Holden) 1115, Central 784 h 5719

Image from the 1902 Chicago City Directory.

Amos and Edwin made a concerted effort to establish themselves in Chicago. The city was an architectural mecca and Amos had a brother who lived there. But the effort faltered in little over a year. For one thing, invited or not, Bessie Russell remained a part of Amos' life and pursued him to the windy city. In 1902, Bessie Russell had Amos arrested for abandonment in Chicago. He was quickly released but the incident was reported in the Grand Rapids Press.

The family struggled on for a few more years before making the decision to move west.

Oil was discovered in Tulsa, Oklahoma, in 1901. This was followed by a much larger finding in 1905 and the rush towards the area was on. The city was made and became known as the "Oil Capital of the World", a long held designation. The construction industry followed the boom. The population escalated and buildings of all purposes and designs were built. The 1910 census taker found Amos, Jessie, Edwin and Delia living together on Lynn Lane in Tulsa.

The timing of the move to Tulsa was ideal for Amos and Edwin. It was a fresh start and a new opportunity. It was an excellent career move. It brought them to a city where no one knew their problems, and placed their skills in the middle of a strong and growing need. They took partners and received important contracts. Within ten years of arriving in Tulsa, they designed its city hall. It felt like a return to normal.

For Delia this new life, this new hope, this step forward, was an ending. They sold the house that Edwin designed, selecting every doorknob himself, and where they lived together as a family until Eddie was six and a half. They gave away Eddie's clothes and toys, his bed.

Everything in Tulsa seemed new, as if it was being invented before her eyes. She had no memories in this city and no one here had any memories of her. No one here knew her as a mother. Even her child's tomb was far away. She lived the rest of her life in Tulsa, until her own death at ninety in 1957. Then she returned to Grand Rapids to join the others in the family mausoleum while the Parbel family lived out the last days of the home that Edwin designed for her and Eddie.

#

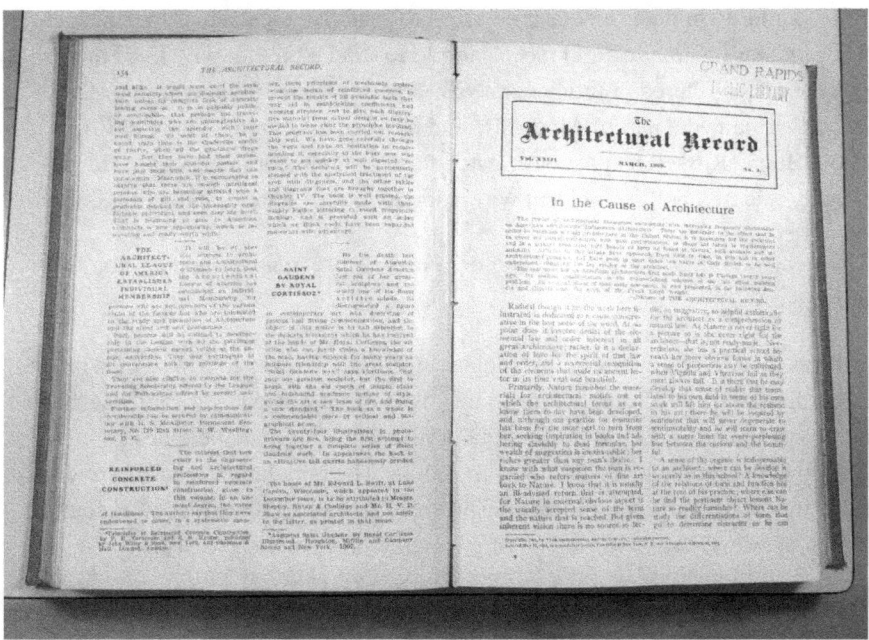

Bruce Goff recalled that Edwin Rush often consulted a copy of this issue of the Architectural Record and otherwise kept it in a locked cabinet. The object of interest was an extensive article about Frank Lloyd Wright's work, containing many images. This copy is in the collection of the Grand Rapids Public Library.

Amos and Edwin worked with Asbury Endacott in Tulsa for over five years before they met Bruce. They were well established in their new city, which is what prompted the meeting.

It was a quiet afternoon at the firm's office that was interrupted by an unexpected visitor. Amos agreed to meet him.

"Would you be Mr. Rush or Mr. Endacott, sir?"

"Amos Rush".

"Good, just who we need to see."

Amos missed the man's name, but registered the shabby suit, the dirty shoes, the slight flush to his face, his nose. The man gave the impression of a salesman who had indulged himself at the saloon over lunch. The curious thing was the grim faced, probably ten or twelve year old boy with him.

Bruce's father, Corliss Goff, rough and mildly drunk, took his son into town one day and boldly knocked unannounced at the office of Rush, Endacott & Rush. Corliss showed Amos drawings his son had made. The Goffs were invited in. Amos declared that the boy had talent and even could be an architect if he wanted. Before they left, arrangements were made for Bruce to begin a part-time apprenticeship in the Rush office. It was a different time.

One day after the apprenticeship started, Bruce sat at a table with a heavy book open before him, a piece of tracing paper and a pencil in hand. Behind him with his feet up on his own desk, Amos flipped through a newspaper humming. By now Bruce knew the "central importance of the Greek orders, like learning the ABCs". They were appearing in Bruce's drawings regularly. They helped him solve problems. But he was growing a little bored with the basics. How many more Doric columns would Amos make him trace?

Just then Amos announced a coffee break for himself and left Bruce with some parting instructions.

Amos spent less time at the firm than the younger men now and often went home for coffee in the afternoon. Bruce's mind quickly wandered after Amos left. He got up to use the bathroom. Edwin's office door was wide open though he and the other men were involved in a meeting in another room.

Bruce stepped in to steal a quick glance. Edwin's office was enticing. There were interesting drawings on the wall, and a table with his tools. There was a cabinet filled with architectural books and journals so precious that it was always kept locked.

Except today, when improbably, the door was open. Of all the times he'd glanced that way, Bruce never expected to see that. He wasn't sure he believed his eyes.

His ears told Bruce that Edwin and the others were down the hall. He would hear them if they stopped talking or if they came his way. He would only look.

One book he recognized by its shape, having often seen Edwin with it. The Architectural Record for January through June 1908 bound together. Bruce would love to know what was in it. Worse than that, he thought he did know. There had been talk around the office about a man named Frank Wright who was doing some things with architecture, the likes of which had never been seen.

Had it grown quiet down the hall? Bruce turned and stepped back towards the door trying to look like someone on an errand. There he heard a lower conversation led by Edwin, a story about some old project in Grand Rapids. Perfect. He was back at the cabinet in a soft leap. He snatched the bound journal and opened it to a spot marked by a slip of paper in the March issue.

He read, "The sentiment for an American architecture first made itself felt in Chicago twenty years ago... An original phase of that early movement is now presented, in the following article and illustrations, the work of Mr. Frank Lloyd Wright." Bruce was stirred. The first page of the piece spoke of a new movement indigenous to the United States, a love of nature and organic influences. Then he turned the pages and there were photographs, many pages of photographs; an office building with exterior and interior images, a curved reception desk, the most exciting looking chairs, globe shaped lights, homes as well with entirely unique shapes and interior spaces, floor plans, drawings of furniture and art...

The outside world intruded suddenly with an extra sensory realization. Bruce jerked forward in his chair and looked around to find Edwin observing him from the doorway. All Bruce could do was stammer, nothing came out right. No excuse would work, he was caught red-handed. Just the corner of Edwin's mouth moved upwards slightly.

"What have you got there?" Edwin asked, but with a softness, not a scold. Edwin stepped around Bruce and placed the pads of three fingers on the page. And then he looked at Bruce with an expression a twelve year old boy would be incapable of reading. Bruce had no knowledge that for six and a half years, Edwin had a little boy of his own who might have grown up and been interested in architecture.

Edwin sat down next to Bruce and they chatted. Bruce had never had such access to Edwin. Edwin told Bruce about Frank Lloyd Wright and also Louis Sullivan. He called them the two greatest practicing American architects. "You should see the mausoleums that Sullivan designed actually." Bruce was awkward in the silence that followed. "Well," Edwin smiled and laid a palm on the table and rose. "You had better get back to your assignment."

Edwin was forty-eight at the time. He was only thirty years old when he designed his own mausoleum.

Bruce Goff would eventually become a prominent and prolific architect.

He drafted the design for the remarkable Boston Avenue Methodist Church in Tulsa in the late 1920s, while still with the Rush firm. He eventually chaired the School of Architecture at the University of Oklahoma. He earned a reputation as a highly innovative designer of homes. Before he died, he shared some glimpses of his childhood and his initiation into his trade, such as the day his father took him to Tulsa to meet the Rushes, and also the day he discovered the work of Frank Lloyd Wright in Edwin Rush's Architectural Journal.

#

This photo of Edwin Rush was found among Bruce Goff's papers at the Art Institute of Chicago. Though the original was not dated, based on his suit and the telephone behind him, it is not likely that it was taken before 1920 when Edwin was 52. (Rush, Edwin A., portrait. Bruce A. Goff Archive, Ryerson and Burnham Archives, The Art Institute of Chicago, Digital File #199001_170403-001.)

One design element remained unfinished on the Rush mausoleum.

Originally the architects envisioned a winged disc over the doorway. Neither Amos nor Edwin realized for some time that their dissatisfaction with this feature was mutual.

In the depth of his mourning, this project with his father to memorialize the child with their art, was Edwin's only means of drawing breath. He realized that Delia did not understand, that she was even hurt by this but he could not relieve her without asphyxiating. Her lack of understanding was hurtful to him in return and the pain coiled around their relationship.

But Amos could relate to Edwin. Both men knew what had to be done for Eddie and that they had to do it. It was Amos whose drawings of the motif first turned into a face. They had closed themselves in their study, separating themselves from the women who then unfortunately believed they were working on a client project. They will see soon enough what we have done, Edwin thought.

He and his father were drawing without speaking. Then Edwin was at the window and when he turned, Amos met his eye. Amos looked almost surprised, as if something had appeared on the sheet before him independently. Edwin joined him and saw that the winged disk had turned into a small angel. He closed his eyes and stood very still for a moment and then they were both drawing, watching each other's work, revising their own.

What they settled on was ideal: angel wings, Eddie's face, a small Roman style helmet. This was no passive, feminine angel. This angel was vital, triumphant. It was personalized. They had resurrected him as a boy king.

Amos had done some intricate stone work over the years. He had even done a grave marker before, a solitary statue in a quiet place he sometimes thought of with a sense of peace for both he and Jessie. This, though, would be a special accomplishment.

The mausoleum went up and Eddie went into it after waiting out construction in a temporary grave. They held the funeral and another ceremony when the boy was reinterred in the Rush designed crypt. The wings on the figure were completed, as was the small helmet. The ball of the head was shaped. Score marks all over it attested to its having been worked by hand into a nearly three-dimensional sculpture. There was the suggestion of ears, as the formation of the helmet necessitated this. There was even the beginning of a right eye, but the face remained unfinished.

At first this could be attributed to the conjoined issues of the fresh pain that surprised Amos as he attempted this likeness and the enormous pressure he placed on himself to make it beautiful and perfect. Then it was life; the American Modern Builder and Bowman, Bessie Russell, Chicago. Then the project was simply buried by time.

During the main events of mourning it seemed acceptable, even preferable, that Eddie's face did not appear. Then it was normal. And then somehow life continued and required effort in entirely new directions. Eventually they moved to Tulsa, leaving the mausoleum in Grand Rapids and the angel to face a featureless future in which no one knew him and no one could see him.

Source Notes

The information available about the death of Edwin Harold Rush (the son and only child of Edwin Arthur and Delia Rush) came from City of Grand Rapids cemetery records (now online at http://grcity.us/parks/Pages/Cemeteries-.aspx), and the death certificate for the child from the Kent County Clerk's office (now online through the Seeking Michigan website: http://seekingmichigan.contentdm.oclc.org/cdm/singleitem/collection/p129401coll7/id/955245/rec/1).

Information about other Rush family struggles came from the following articles:

"Rush Didn't Stay." Grand Rapids Press. July 6, 1895.

"Must Not Interfere." Grand Rapids Herald. June 17, 1900.

"Claims A.W. Rush." Grand Rapids Press. July 28, 1902.

The stories about Bruce Goff came from the following book:

DeLong, David Gilson. The Architecture of Bruce Goff. (New York: Garland Publishing Inc., 1977)

The article about Frank Lloyd Wright in the architectural journal that fascinated both Goff and Edwin Rush was:

"In the Cause of Architecture." The Architectural Journal. March 1908.

General information about the family came from obituaries, city directories, school board proceedings; cemetery, census and vital records.

Images in this chapter are individually credited in captions.

The First Day of
Summer Vacation

Ruth stands near her mother who is holding Marvin at the front steps of the Marshall Street home. Photo courtesy of Ruth VanStee.

One slip of a story about the Rush mausoleum, a memory from childhood, a scene, really, shared with me by my coworker soon after I first discovered the monument was particularly exciting. Ruth was the one in favor of my initial adventure with Caitlin. She tipped me into doing it. So afterwards, I naturally gushed to her about the way it turned out. She responded equally strongly. She got a sudden, intense look on her face and froze briefly, like some character from a Dragnet episode.

"I know that mausoleum," she said.

She played there as a child. She grew up in the neighborhood. Already I was hooked. Here was a witness to the transformation, to the fall. Even if she never dropped her bombshell about the difference in the Rush mausoleum evident fifty years ago, I still would have wanted to know more about her childhood in the area around the cemetery.

The houses in Ruth's neighborhood, called Oakdale, were built before the war and the children were born after it. There were plenty of children. They appeared in bunches like fireworks celebrating armistice; three pregnant women on one street, two baby girls on the same block, the next class at church.

Ruth's home was on Marshall Street and her mother and father were Rose and Herman VanHouten. Both Rose and Herman came from Dutch families, as was the case for most of the people in the neighborhood. Rose's family arrived in America more recently and Herman's, from a different part of the old country considered higher Dutch, had been on this side of the ocean for generations.

Rose worked as a domestic, day work, before the marriage and continued to do some cleaning and sometimes took in wash after marrying and having children. Herman was a carpenter. He served briefly as a medic for the Air Force during the War, discharged within a year due to the discovery of a hearing problem. Afterwards he always wore a hearing aid and his uniform hung in the hall closet upstairs.

Their first child, Jan, was born in 1944. Rich followed two years later. Ruth came onto the scene in 1949 and Marvin finished the foursome in 1952. Their home was two stories with an open staircase off the living room. There was a landing upstairs big enough for the children to play blind man's bluff on, with built-in cupboards. The two girls shared a bedroom and so did the boys.

They virtually lived on the screened front porch in the summer, sleeping there on hot nights and otherwise sitting there as often as they sat. This was the social extension of the home, where they met the neighborhood. They planted a maple near the front walk to someday help shade the porch and the house. There was a flower garden in the shape of a figure eight in the side yard, Herman had the touch for roses; and a vegetable garden in back. There was a row of hollyhocks along the side of the house that bordered the alley.

The VanDykes, an older couple, lived on the other side of the alley. They had a wide driveway, ideal for playing jump rope, and a quite outstanding garden. The children could sneak rhubarb through the fence. The VanDykes, who no longer had young children at home, making them a slight anomaly, were generally tolerant of these intrusions from their small neighbors and had not overreacted the time Ruth's yo-yo sailed through their glass window.

The children went to Oakdale Christian School, a few blocks northeast and the family attended Oakdale Park Christian Reformed Church, one block directly east. On the corners of both Eastern and Kalamazoo streets, the main north/south thoroughfares to their east and west, were the commercial buildings they relied on to supply their staples. A block north and east was Korfiker, the grocer, who Ruth sometimes observed still packing a box with an order for delivery. A block straighter east, another grocer, Haan, was where they bought their meat. Two blocks southwest, at Oakdale and Eastern was Kuizema Hardware, a pharmacy, Wierenga's service station. A little off the corner, so they funneled through an alley to access it, was the East End Creamery where ice cream cones cost a nickel.

Farther afield were further options. The bank and Van's Pastry were a few blocks north. At Madison and Hall was one of the city's earliest suburban shopping centers. Eventually both Ruth and her sister would work the soda fountain and lunch counter at the drugstore there, their main customer base being the men from the Oldsmobile dealership across the road. Each major or minor intersection offered its own major or minor institutions. The possibilities for variety were limited only by your feet or bicycle tires.

Equally accessible were the places for the children to play. Their own street with its steep hill coming down from Hall, was the best for sliding when they could avoid traffic, which was most of the time. Her own or another older brother often organized baseball games from the pickings of the five and six children

Ruth's childhood home on Marshall Street in the Oakdale neighborhood. Photo courtesy of Ruth VanStee.

families in the surrounding homes. To even the playing field, a ball that went over the Viersen's house across the street was an automatic out. While their own Oakdale Christian school playground was small, Oakdale public school, an equal distance in the opposite direction, had a new park school facility with swings and big sandboxes. Beyond it, the lumber yards were an open stage for forming imaginary camps. Franklin Park, a city park with tennis courts and a swimming pool, was a short bike ride away.

Then, of course, there was the over sixty-five acre open space with trees and hills and grass and winding lanes, uncluttered with automobile traffic, one block to the west of Ruth's house. The children could not resist Oakhill cemetery. It was a major feature of the neighborhood and their lives. It was a place of freedom and intrigue for youthful imaginations.

It was natural that the children would find themselves there often. I loved Ruth's stories about Oakdale neighborhood, loved thinking of it in its former glory, loved the casual extravagance of a Victorian cemetery in the middle of it. The most compelling thing she ever told me, though, came that day when I first told her about my visit with Caitlin.

She remembered the Rush mausoleum because when she was a child, the door was open.

It was the only structure in the cemetery with an open door and this was irresistible to her and her friends. The children dared each other to touch the door, fleeing in the opposite direction as soon as they did. Ruth remembered seeing curled, dry leaves on the floor.

For me this was as tantalizing as it was for the children. She got me almost there. I could see down on that floor through her memories, but I couldn't look around at the rest of the interior.

I was left with imagining.

I picture the first day of summer vacation:

Technically it was spring, and it felt like it that morning. There was a thunderstorm the night before and now the world felt freshly washed. The children were out early and the sun was filtering through damp leaves onto damp grass. A bird sang nearby as though it was dawn.

Open Mausoleum Door

Ruth was standing in front of the Rush mausoleum, girding for the dare.

Something larger than dead leaves and stone drawers unnerved her, something larger than her understanding. There was a presence within the mausoleum like static electricity. She braced for the shock, or more the catch, the pull towards it, towards some terrifying connection, humanity's greatest paradox.

Considering the figure above the door, it was a literal face off, and a profound one. Flesh faced stone, both equally fragile and indestructible. One child was simultaneously rooted to the present and a manifestation of timelessness, the first day of summer vacation being attended by the disappearance of all those limits that implied time. The other was rooted to the past but had achieved immortality through the ordinary process. One child had muscle and limbs and her run of the neighborhood. The other had wings and had escaped all earthly boundaries.

Ruth made her run. With her left fingertips she reached out, into the sensation, for the solidity of the door. As if the children with her would know, she attended to the validity of the contact.

For a moment she was met by a force that projected itself toward life just as she projected herself toward what is beyond this life. For a moment she was reached by the longing for what is precious in a child. She shared energy with something unseen.

And then she escaped. Her heels came down, her waist swiveled and her head turned. The vertigo reversed and the presence reluctantly released its arms.

Ruth survived. Standing panting near the back of the group of children while someone else took their turn, she looked around her to a field of other doors now looking back at her. Some of the feeling of a presence, a pull, returned to her and it became clear that sometimes, a closed door is the same as an open one.

Ruth reached her late teens during the height of the civil rights era and graduated from Central Christian High in 1967. The world and the neighborhood were changing by then. Martin Luther King Jr. came as close as Chicago. The local Urban League and NAACP fought local realtors over discrimination and lead workshops for minority people trying to buy houses. A black family moved into a home just north of her, near Franklin Park.

That did cause a buzz among her Dutch neighbors.

Many of them were getting older now and were no longer the newcomers, the ones struggling for a foothold. It was less unusual for the houses in Ruth's neighborhood to be occupied only by an old couple. That plump bouquet of children that once ran these streets was growing up. Ruth herself was looking forward to starting at Calvin soon, the city's Christian Reformed college. She would live at home as many did, but just as many were finding their way away.

The houses in the neighborhood continued to age, too. Some of the older people had trouble maintaining them like they used to. They were forgiven for this, of course. Eventually they solved the problem by moving places that required little in the way of upkeep. Ruth's dad, a man of few words, complained once that he was seldom able to step outside to do his yard work now and end up in a conversation with someone he knew well.

Ruth hardly noticed the changes. They were so gradual and this was her home. She was barely aware of the plan to sell her Christian high school for a public middle school. Opposition from the local black leadership was strong. The Grand Rapids Press reported the complaint from Rev. Albert Keith from Messiah Baptist Church to the school board, "The fundamental problem is that you are not helping us (the Negro community) at all in the problem of segregation."

Though Ruth attended a school every day that was strictly white, Dutch, Christian Reformed, if it were made public, it would be all black. This was the neighborhood. The truth was that for a time Ruth lived in a carefully balanced world. The "Negro community" was physically fairly close to her but socially quite cleanly separate. They lived in clusters just south of downtown, just west of Ruth. They had their own commercial establishments, their own schools close to them, like South High School. South was overcrowded now and a middle school would alleviate the problem. Not the problem of segregation, though.

Black people hoping to escape the ghetto came up against White people who were afraid that Black people would bring the ghetto with them. There were programs now to assist people of color to improve their housing and living conditions but the very programs meant to help, fledgling and inadequate as they were, imposed a stigma that added to the harm. Almost simultaneous to the appearance of these programs was the accusation from a segment of the dominant culture that Black people were relying on handouts. Realtors and bankers actively fought integration, sometimes openly by banding together to oppose regulation and sometimes surreptitiously by drawing a red line on a map or making a fearful suggestion under their breath to a homeowner.

Certainly things were bound to get better now, in this day of peace and love, this era of enlightenment.

In the summer of 1967, the Grand Rapids police chased a group of Black men in an allegedly stolen car. The men ditched the car and ran. When the police caught up to them, one of the men from the car fell and onlookers could see he was wearing a cast. It was a warm day in an area near crowded bars, so there was an audience. A two-day period of violence followed with fights in the street, looting of businesses and buildings burned to the ground, almost exclusively in the central black neighborhood. This open unrest left a lasting scar. The next year, Martin Luther King Jr. was assassinated.

I seem to have a tendency here in the mid-century, to introduce new people to the story.

If I were going to go back to that same first day of summer vacation, I could glance away from Ruth and her friends at the Rush mausoleum for a moment toward an older boy riding his bicycle north of them from his home in East Grand Rapids towards downtown. He liked to visit the public museum on Jefferson. There were Indian artifacts laid out in rows and an enormous whale skeleton hung from the ceiling.

On his way he passed through vast neighborhoods of huge Victorian homes. They fascinated him already at this age.

Another ten years would go by before John would walk here as an adult with his own son, a namesake, and step up onto the porch of one of these homes, press his forehead against the front window for a look inside and act on his interest. That is his real point of intersection with the story.

John Logie and his three-year-old namesake son stood on a corner in Grand Rapids admiring a gorgeous old home with impressive stonework. It was the perfect afternoon for a stroll. The spring of 1969 was progressing into summer. It was time for the boys to escape the apartment.

The Logies were just returning from a period of several years away. Both John and Susie were born in Grand Rapids. John was the fourth generation in his family to be. But he'd spent the past eleven years serving in the navy, both on destroyers in the Pacific and teaching at the Naval Academy, and then attended the University of Michigan in Ann Arbor.

In Annapolis, John was surrounded by history and historic landmarks and there was an active preservation movement. The National Historic Preservation Act of 1966 resulted in a National Register of Historic Places. Within the first year, Annapolis had its state capital, a historic district with 120 18th century buildings and the Naval Academy itself, among other sites, listed on the register. John always loved the aesthetic of old architecture, the importance of its testimony, and Annapolis only fueled his existing belief in the hope of saving it.

Now he was back to the home of his childhood, the city where his father, grandfather and great-grandfathers stood in buildings and walked the sidewalks and participated in community before him. His little boy stirred beside him and John looked down. Sometimes his namesake reminded him so much of himself he had to wonder how their lives would parallel or if, in fact, they were simply variations of the same life created by a natural world that seemed to like that game. Perhaps everything was variation of one life.

They came from their apartment on Madison, near downtown. So much had changed from the downtown of John's childhood. The city center became a ghost of itself after the suburbs flourished, with vacant shops and restaurants, new location signs, broken windows. Though the blocks were still crowded with diverse architecture, there was an attempt to obliterate historic features. Ornate, upper story windows were boarded up. Architectural detail was hidden in plain site with a wash of monotone grey or beige paint. Some buildings were sheathed partially or entirely with new facades. At the same time, modern signage shouting in the accent of contemporary design tried to divert attention away from any sign of age.

But even more ambitious modifications were underway. The vision in the minds of many was to start over, to build something new and different, to break from the past, to eliminate the past, to tear it all down.

Hundreds of homes came down for the interstates. And soon the city center that had dimmed was being virtually leveled. Twelve whole blocks in the middle of the city were reduced to pale sand and bulldozer tire tracks. Over a hundred and twenty buildings were pulled down just within this core; Italianate commercial buildings, four theaters, a brewery with a high relief of two horses heads on the front of its stables.

This photo was taken during the height of urban renewal. The view is looking northeast past Immanuel Lutheran Church with the bulldozers at work in the foreground.

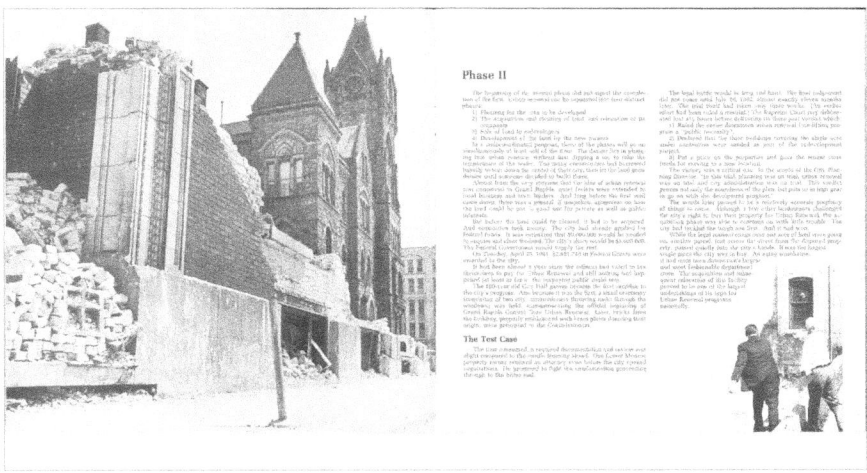

Pages from an urban renewal report showing and describing city commissioners throwing rocks through windows of the Grand Rapids City Hall garage as a kick off for the project. (Coll. 222, Box 1)

The movement was called urban renewal. It was a program to stop inner city deterioration and eradicate blight. The federal government supported it with major funding and the city leaders were committed to it. When a sizable federal grant came through, the city commission celebrated with a small ceremony during which they were photographed throwing rocks through the windows of the city hall garage.

There were a few hold-outs; folks who wanted to keep their existing businesses, their buildings, their neighborhoods. They declared opposition, wouldn't sell out their heritage. Their struggles were perceived and described as threats to progress. They each lost their fights in swift succession with little suspense. A force emanated from behind the desks in upper floor offices, set to work by government officials and the business community, which ultimately produced a legal recourse to simply take and destroy the buildings anyway.

Now this force had its sight set on the homes of the once luxurious hill district just outside of downtown. Many of the fine old lumber baron's mansions were carved up into apartments in the post war grab for housing and no longer maintained with the same reverence as in the past, many in the possession of absentee landlords. Cars were accumulating in the streets, lawns becoming overgrown, roofs taking on moss.

In the middle of all of this, John and his little boy were looking at a house.

The recent riots came quite close. Empty lots where buildings burned were just a few blocks south.

"Look at that old beauty," John said.

They were standing at the corner of Union and Cherry facing northeast. It was not the first time he'd noticed this house. In fact, it was a favorite of his since he'd ridden his bike through here as a boy. He knew that it was built by a prominent local lumberman, Thomas Friant, designed by father and son architects named Rush.

This thing was really far out. The upper story window looked like something from a European castle. Well, that and the turret, and those were leaded glass windows in the turret. There was a thick ring of high bushes enclosing the place and limiting the view, but the house had the inexplicable look of being unoccupied.

STREET FI'S

RES Castle-Type $ 36,500   DIRECT'S N.E. Cor. of Union   601 Cherry, S. E.   St.

No. Bdrms. 4   TERMS Cash

7-16-69   456-1777   **C 2818**   OWNER Dr./Mrs. C. D. Webb

GEORGE A. MILLER, REALTOR

E. VanPopering EM-1-8205   ADD/ZIP 833 Lake Dr., S. E.

PH Res   Bus GL 1-2689

Leg. Desc. Lots 1 & 2 Kelloggs' Sub.

☐ Twp. ☐ City   Lot Sz. 132 x 132

Rooms (16 rooms) Vest., LR, DR, Library, Pantry, ref. room, Kit.-Bath 4 BDRMs, Dressing room-3 Baths   Baths 4½   Garage Carriage House

Fire'pl. 5   Dr. Priv. Yes Pty.

Est. Age Old   Shows Well   Swim Pool No   Water Front No

Porch Front-Back   Sch. Gr Fountain

Heat Steam Fuel Gas   Built of Brick&Stone   Why Sell Liquidating   Sch. Jr. Central

Gas Yes   Bsm't Full   Trade No   Sch. High Central

In Use ☒ Pub Water ☒ Pub Sewer ☐ Well ☐ Septic   St. Pav'd Yes   Paroch

In Street (Not Connected) ☐ Sewer ☐ Water   Assm'ts None   Blks. Gr. Sch. 4

Blt. Ins: ☐ Dish ☐ Disp. ☐ R/O   Est. Taxes 879.40 v. 12,000   Blks. City Bus at door

Debt Type F & C $ @   % +   % $ Mo. Incl. ☐ tax ☐ ins. Held By

Remarks: Large mirror in upper S.W. BR reserved. Also etched windows on stairway.

To Show Call L. O.   Poss. Date 5 days a/c   Zoned B-2

The above information is subject to verification and no liability for errors or omissions is assumed by the listing or selling office.

These real estate listing cards were created by realtors before the digital era. This is the one John Logie would have seen when he purchased the former Friant home.

He lifted Johnnie into his arms, what could be more innocent than a man out for a stroll with his three-year-old, and slid past the bushes up the walk. Soon after, they actually had their faces pressed against the windows. Sure enough, the house was mostly empty. The view was partially obstructed by curtains or structure but he caught compelling glimpses of parquet flooring, a fireplace with an ornamental screen, a built in oak buffet with a mirror, leaf patterned brass light fixtures.

The carriage house, also architecturally unique, beckoned from the back yard and next he was bold enough to slip around the side of the home towards it and explore the less public side of the property.

On his way back toward the sidewalk, he dropped to his knees and peered in a basement window and then his smile disappeared. Water. A fair amount of it.

He and Johnnie hurried away.

He did check the tax rolls to learn the owner the next chance he had. It was Dr. Clarence Webb, 'Spider', they called him. John knew him, worked as an orderly for Webb in the fifties. He started talking to neighbors, mutual acquaintances. The house was previously owned by a man named Richard Davies for decades, but Davies died just months before the riots and his family, glad to be rid of it, sold to Webb.

Webb hadn't moved in but hosted a Christmas party at the home just about the time John and Susie were getting back to GR, Christmas 1968, and never properly sealed off the water afterwards. It didn't matter, Webb just planned to demolish the old thing. He bought it for the property, planned to put up a new medical office building, something cinder block like the one directly kitty corner and others now showing up on the street.

In the meantime, John met a woman named Linda DeJong. Linda was the president of a neighborhood association for folks in the Hill district that they just started the summer before. She lived in a big old gorgeous house on Prospect that she loved. She loved the neighborhood, too, and it bothered her that it was being discounted. She invited a few friends who lived nearby to her home one weekend and the subject came up.

"They think the only people living downtown anymore are transients, hippies or prisoners of the system," she told the group. "We need a way to spread the word about what we have here. Otherwise, it's going to be too late and we might as well all pack up and leave." Ideas got tossed around and Linda went to bed that night with some possibilities in mind.

One of the others who was at her house that weekend gave the group the name Heritage Hill Association. The Press reported that the group had formed and was encouraging folks in the neighborhood to fly flags on the fourth of July and leave porch lights on at night in order to "add a cheery touch to the area".

John and Susie started attending the meetings and getting involved with the group. Few of them could have predicted how fast things were about to change.

Dr. Webb left for a vacation in the Bahamas and the Friant house continued to sit empty. In the Bahamas, Webb posed for a photo in front of a beautiful scene. Behind the camera, his wife, Maxine, tried to frame him just right as he stood at the top of a cliff, a long view spreading out in the background. "Step back just a little," she coached and his eyes on her, he complied. "Just a little more, " Maxine instructed as she focused on the complicated controls of the sophisticated equipment. While she squinted at the zoom, Spider tripped and flailing, fell backwards.

The Heritage Hill Association quickly began attracting a good sized group to their meetings, often over a hundred. They got the idea for a home tour to promote their neighborhood. If folks who didn't know much about the hill district could be attracted to just walk through some of its lovely, old houses, could see the workmanship in the unique features of older architecture, could see how the homes were maintained and loved by their families, then maybe they would gain a little respect for the neighborhood.

In the meantime a College Park project threatened whole blocks of homes on the north side of Heritage Hill. It was a plan by the city's board of education to expand their downtown junior college into a campus that stretched eastward to meet Central High School. The project had been in the planning stages for several years now, since the fall of 1966, while funding was sought. It would involve taking out at least thirty old homes in an area that was portrayed as blighted and hopeless.

The irony was not lost on anyone at the new Heritage Hill Neighborhood Association that it was the project leaders who were purchasing those homes and neglecting them. That was just the most prominent project among others to set its intentions on destruction in the neighborhood.

Linda DeJong offered her house for the home tour. So did Barb Roelofs, another very active member of the association. With the collaboration of other resource folks, plans came along nicely and the group hoped to attract a few hundred to the tour.

Fifteen hundred people came to the first Heritage Hill Neighborhood home tour in May of 1969.

Not among them were the Webbs. Spider's fall in the Bahamas was a significant one and his recuperation from his injuries would take some time. His life and his priorities changed in the process and he lost his interest in a medical office building. This made him more approachable by the persistent John Logie, though John's offer of forty thousand dollars for the home and the three lot piece was not enough. The Friant house went on the market.

John coaxed him, "Well at least list me as a prior contact, Spider."

The members of the Heritage Hill Neighborhood Association went to work. They started planning a second home tour for the fall. They held bake sales and put together a calendar with photos of old homes. They went door to door to talk to residents within their designated boundaries. They started a neighborhood watch and offered to help folks with home repairs. They attended realtors meetings to learn and to fight redlining. They contacted local politicians.

The Friant house was up for sale a month before Spider agreed to John's offer. The Logies had to agree to the jump in interest rates that took place during the month. John also had to agree to pay Spider off in five years. They had twenty five hundred from the GI bill to put down on a land contract, so that would be quite a trick. They would have to get a loan, and loans were very hard to come by for folks that wanted to buy in the hill district. Linda DeJong couldn't get a loan on her house.

This is where John's background came in handy for both him and the neighborhood association. He studied law at the U of M, worked as an attorney in Grand Rapids. He negotiated a stipulation in the land contract with Spider. If the Logies couldn't pay off the house in five years and they could offer written proof that they tried to get a loan and were denied, Spider had to give them another five years.

The first thing the preservationists had to do to prevent the College Park project from tearing through Heritage Hill was to designate the neighborhood a historic district. And the first major obstacle toward that goal was the fact that there was no law enabling local historic districts in the state of Michigan. This was the kind of thing John was trained and experienced at tackling. He and others went to work on an appropriate state law. The College Park project boosters had no such preliminary work to do, they were years ahead of the preservationists.

Meanwhile there were losses. John Ball was one of Grand Rapid's pioneers who distinguished himself as an explorer traveling as widely as Oregon, Hawaii and Cape Horn. He built a home on the four hundred block of the Fulton Street hill, surrounded by beautiful, elaborate residences belonging to other prominent citizens. In 1965 it was demolished and a small, nondescript apartment building put in its place.

In early November 1969, the Grand Rapids City Hall, a magnificent building that was the focal point of the city center, designed by the same architect who conceived the Michigan state capital, was destroyed by a wrecking crew in an urban renewal initiative. It was replaced with surface parking.

John Logie and the Heritage Hill Association proceeded with the work on the state enabling law, but that was only one focus of their efforts. Acting as though success at the state would come, they drafted a local historic district ordinance and they took it to the city ordinance committee. In turn the city was willing to allow for the possibility of success at the state. They were willing to give the process a chance – for six months. The ordinance committee placed a temporary moratorium on demolition within the boundaries this new neighborhood association had designated for itself.

For a moment, for Heritage Hill, the bulldozers were forced to pause.

The preservationists on the hill did not.

Next they went after designation on the national register of historic places. Two consultants from Washington were sent to Grand Rapids to survey the homes in Heritage Hill. They combed the streets, taking photos and notes and looking at over twelve hundred homes. Hill residents helped. One woman became a regular in the public library's local history department, using its Sanborn maps and city directories and old newspapers to supply important names and dates. The consultants reported on every house in the neighborhood and identified sixty distinct architectural styles and five hundred homes exhibiting exemplary architectural status.

The city extended the moratorium on demolition another six months. Then they did it again, continually.

In 1971, after two years of steady work, the Heritage Hill Neighborhood was placed on the National Register of Historic Places. With the designation came certain protections. Whether those protections would hold any weight was the next issue. The neighbors had to keep a watch for what they called "midnight demolitions".

Grand Rapids City Hall mid-demolition in 1969. Several urban renewal era buildings have already gone up around it.

The National Historic Preservation Act of 1966 did stipulate that anyone receiving federal funding for projects that involved demolishing old homes was subject to a local hearing to review the impact of their plans. While this helpful safeguard existed on paper, it had never yet actually been called into use. It would have its first test in Grand Rapids, Michigan. The College Park project relied on federal funds. John and the group from the hill asked for their hearing.

The land contract with Spider was settled but John and Susie still couldn't move into their house. It wasn't in any condition. They stayed in the apartment and got a short term loan to fix their new home's plumbing and wiring, though this was not moving them closer to the goal of paying off the land contract in five years. In five years, the Logies felt like they were just hanging on to the house, just able to make the monthly payments. There were two more members of the family. They adopted a daughter and then another daughter came along the following year, the final year of the land contract.

John was a partner in his law firm by then. He had both a secure job and some valuable contacts. So he approached a bank with a long history in Grand Rapids, like the Logie family itself. The bank was also one of two major clients of John's own firm.

They denied the loan. "We don't make mortgages in that area," the loan officer told him.

"Listen, Al, we can turn this neighborhood around. My family and I, we're not going anywhere. We walk the kids to school – heck, they don't go outside without one of us. We have good locks on the doors. But we love this house, we all do, this is our home now, and it's gonna be. And we're not the only ones. This neighborhood is full of people, some of them have been there for years and will be for years to come."

"You're putting obstacles in our way. You're working against us. How are these people, and I'm one of them, supposed to even do the basic upkeep when they don't have access to the simple credit that any homeowner needs?"

John broke off when Al, generally polite and patient, let his gaze slip toward his receptionist for the second time. "Am I keeping you from another appointment, Al?"

"Nope, nope, all the time in the world," Al forced a smile.

John sighed.

Then he explained his arrangement with Spider. "Would you write me a letter, decline me in a letter, then?"

John got the letter that day.

The President of the second bank that John applied to for a mortgage had regularly hired John specifically, not just John's firm, as his attorney.

This man also turned John down. And this man was also willing to admit his refusal in writing.

Despite his position and his contacts, John could not get a mortgage. He was, however, because of his quick thinking, able to hold on to his home. Spider had no choice but to extend the land contract for the agreed upon additional five years. Something would have to change by then, though. John and Susie were all the more resolved to fight redlining.

"I'm going to have to talk to my supervisor", the deputy general counsel of HUD told John from across the desk in the Washington, D.C. office. John had been working his way up the chain of command for weeks now and explained several times along the way why the federal agency must not grant money to the College Park project in downtown Grand Rapids. "These developers are supposed to study the impact of their project on our neighborhood. They're supposed to explore alternatives. I can tell you they haven't done any of that and yet they're planning to demolish dozens of old homes right in the middle of an established, vibrant..." he inhaled and leaned back in his chair and softened his voice.

"And if this is the right thing for the community, for the citizens of Grand Rapids, then the conference will make that clear to everyone involved once and for all. In any case, section 106 of the NHPA entitles us to a compliance conference."

Now John sat in the office alone squinting at a bad painting and preparing himself for a further fight. He was the legal representative for Heritage Hill by then and he paid for this trip to Washington himself. Defenses for his position passed through his mind in phrases, "been on the national register for a year", "like knocking the front tooth out of this neighborhood".

Members of the Heritage Hill Association (from left Barbara Roelofs, Linda DeJong and John Logie) look at the new publication, "The Homes of Heritage Hill" in April 1970. Photo courtesy of the Davenport University Archives.

Eventually the deputy general counsel reappeared with another man in a suit. John tried to confirm for himself that this was now the general counsel of HUD while at the same time gauging the new man's attitude, his shifting gaze, his impatient posture.

His intentions became clear quickly, however, when he spoke. "Now listen, we don't really know what this section 106 means," then he stopped briefly and looked at the floor with his hands on his hips, "but if it means anything, it means you get your conference."

"Would you be willing to write a letter to that effect, sir?"

And sometimes it worked like this, John mused as he traveled home to Grand Rapids, the game changing letter from the head of HUD's legal division tucked into his briefcase. Sometimes the bureaucrat in the suit decided in your favor. If you worked to create a foundation, a construct for them, sometimes the person with the right authority, followed your logic and supported you. Each number of an intricate combination lined up and a door opened, and an entire community progressed through. That's why John dedicated his career to the law, because sometimes it worked like this.

If there was any chance of making progress in society, you all had to do your job. You had to get up on Monday morning and go to work. You had to stop and manage all the details and the setbacks, and work together. You had to behave civilly when you disagreed and get face to face and talk through it.

That is not easy, none of it is.

Sometimes you did all that work and did not achieve your goal. Sometimes you did achieve your goal only to realize that didn't solve your problems.

Logie and the Heritage Hill Association succeeded in stopping the College Park project from going through as originally intended and wiping out blocks of old homes in the neighborhood. After the second five years that Logie bought himself to pay off his home, he had no problem securing a loan.

It wasn't just the homes in the neighborhood that were saved, but the community. John became the president of the PTA where his kids went to school, for example, and in response to this kind of social involvement by the neighborhood association, the property values kept rising.

Today Heritage Hill is a thriving, widely considered desirable, neighborhood. They still do a home tour every year. Attendees enjoy getting into some of the impressive old places and seeing what the owners have done with them. It is a popular event, except of course, among those who don't like crowds.

John Logie was elected mayor of Grand Rapids in 1992. He served three terms, accomplishing a great deal for the city. He was especially appreciated by folks in the local history community.

He died in 2021, but Susie still owns the home that Amos and Edwin Rush designed for Thomas Friant, still maintains it beautifully. A few years ago, it received a fresh coat of paint in a handsome new color that got a lot of attention. Most recently, she erected a large banner in the front yard protesting the police killing of a young Black man in Grand Rapids.

And right around the corner from the Logies now is my other guide to the mid-century.

At Calvin, Ruth got serious with a boy she knew from high school and they married in 1970 just before each receiving their teaching certificates.

Ruth and Duff raised their children in Oakdale neighborhood which Ruth described as a "nice community, nicely integrated". Their children went to the same Oakdale school as Ruth and her siblings but now many of the teachers were African Americans. After Ruth's dad died in 1977, her mom stayed in the neighborhood for some time and continued to attend Oakdale church which had black pastors by then.

For all that John Logie and his Heritage Hill neighbors had to overcome in order to save their homes and improve their district, they successfully accessed resources that were simply inaccessible to the people of color settling Oakdale.

Occasionally Ruth and Duff looked at larger, older homes in Eastown or Ottawa Hills. But she said they wanted their kids to be able to walk to school. So it wasn't until the last two were taking the bus anyway, that Ruth and Duff moved. They ended up in Heritage Hill, literally just around the corner from the Logies.

I visited her there when she told me about growing up in Oakdale and playing in front of the Rush mausoleum, the one that was as irresistible to children then, as it was to my red haired niece when I visited fifty years later.

Source Notes

The main inspiration and information for this chapter came from the following two interviews:

Personal interview with Ruth Van Stee, October 22, 2010.

Personal interview with John Logie, June 11, 2010 now in the Grand Rapids Public Library Oral History Collection (Coll. 164, Box 4, #131).

Other information came from the following sources:

"First Progress Report on New JC." Grand Rapids Press. October 4, 1966.

"School Critics Cry 'Ghetto'." Grand Rapids Press. February 7, 1967.

"Hill Association Plans Rejuvenation of Area." Grand Rapids Press. June 25, 1968.

"Group Would Save Area Landmarks." Grand Rapids Press. February 27, 1969.

"City Gets $4.9 Million for Hill Area Project." Grand Rapids Press. July 2, 1969.

"150 Protest Plans for City's College Park Renewal Project." Grand Rapids Press. December 10, 1969.

"City, School Officials Accused of 'Planning Blight' in Project." Grand Rapids Press. February 4, 1971.

"Irate Hill Group Bypasses City to Meet." Grand Rapids Press. May 6, 1971.

"Schoolmen Suspicious of Heritage Hill Talks." Grand Rapids Press. July 7, 1971.

"College Park is a Whole New Ball Game." Grand Rapids Press. July 28, 1971.

"A Taste of Anarchy." the Paper. February 4-10, 1999.

"The Last 40." Grand Rapids Magazine online feature, 2003.

A series of articles appeared in the Heritage Herald (The Newsletter of Heritage Hill), during the association's 30th anniversary in 1998

Heritage Hill Association website, heritagehillweb.org

Central Core - North Urban Renewal Project No. Mich. R-60, Grand Rapids Buildings Collection (Coll. #254, Box 3, Folder 91)

Olson, Gordon. Grand Rapids: A City Renewed. (Grand Rapids: Grand Rapids Historical Commission, 1996)

Images courtesy of the Grand Rapids History Center, Grand Rapids Public Library, Grand Rapids, MI, unless otherwise noted in the photo captions.

Today

Author photo of the Rush monument in Oakwood Cemetery in Lowell, Michigan.

About the time they eliminated the archivist's position at the public library I started doing a couple things that would surprise folks who knew me. I started to run. Okay if you knew me that might even shock you. I've never been much of an athlete. But like everyone I wanted to get in shape and like everyone, that was getting harder for me and I wondered how that would change if I got involved in what I considered this most extreme activity.

The first experiment involved trying to just run around my own block. I started out as slow as I could, to see how it felt, to find a realistic pace that I could sustain. I figured I could speed up as I went.

I made it to the second turn before I was completely out of breath and had to stop.

After that, I decided running was too hard and I didn't do it again for something like a year. Then I got the urge to just try my original goal again. That time I made it all the way around the block and it felt pretty amazing. I think that first victory, as ridiculously humble as it was, had a powerful impact.

In Hollywood we would now flash forward to the gritty finish of my first marathon. I like Hollywood movies, but I just can't get my life to work like one. In fact, my life often fails to show evidence of plot. I can say that I've had some cool experiences running. I run short distances slow and I still get a disproportionate sense of joy in my accomplishments. Better runners often admire my enthusiasm. I did a 10k at the River Bank Run three years in a row. For a period of about a year, I set my alarm for 5:00 am and did a short run in the dark before work. The stars were just amazing the first time out. More recently I was part of a seven person relay team that ran one hundred miles non-stop, sleeping and eating trail mix in an overstuffed van in between our spurs.

But I've also set meaningful goals that I've failed to achieve. When it comes to running, I'm a pretty confirmed "also ran". Running is hard. And boring. And rather extravagantly time consuming. And I do very much enjoy not running.

Maybe the best thing about running for me is that I understand it as a metaphor now.

My career felt like that. I was out there on the trail huffing and puffing but I wasn't seeing the expected milestones. I had some great experiences, for sure, but couldn't say that I was getting where I wanted to get.

And writing felt like that.

So that other thing I started to do after they eliminated the archivist at the local history department was write. I can't truly say 'started' in this case. I've been writing since I was a little girl, things like diary entries and pointless stories about popular girls with boyfriends, all of which I inevitably destroyed in bitter embarrassment. They ended up where they deserved to be. I've heard this is a common progression. Those first efforts are fairly juvenile and you decide you aren't any good. It didn't stop me from writing. I knew it was something I needed and loved to do. It did, however, stop me from believing that anything I generated had value in the real world. It was a secret hobby. No effort at creative writing ever made it beyond the eyes of friends or family.

I learned along the way to write in a more socially acceptable way. I developed an academic or professional style when I needed it for school and work. After finding the Rushes, I wrote more traditional articles about their architecture and about urban development for the Grand Rapids Historical Society magazine, and developed a presentation for local groups.

But as I researched the Rushes, what I found was drama and irony and I wanted to tell that story.

By the time I read the entry for Amos in the Spring Funeral home records, I knew that he, the family patriarch, was the second one to be placed in their mausoleum and his six-year-old grandchild was the first.

One of the initial calls I made about the Rushes yielded the names of the people in the mausoleum, the five people. I knew about Amos and Edwin, and Jessie and Delia, but a cemetery employee added, "Edwin Harold, baby, died September 11, 1898". My introduction to him was the fact of his untimely death.

He lived between the federal censuses and died well before his parents' deaths (and obituaries). Few notations about his existence, one in the cemetery record and a second I was soon to discover, place him in history.

Delia and Edwin lost their only child in a home that is less than a block from where the Helen DeVos Children's Hospital stands in my life.

It wouldn't happen today. Eddie would live.

I thought about what it was like for Delia to return to the site of her life's greatest tragedy after so many years; what it was like for Edwin to stand before his monument to his only child's death as he grieved his father.

I wondered how Eddie's death affected the couple. We hear that it's not unusual for a marriage to struggle or fail after such a loss. I could easily imagine an estrangement from each other, from life. The entire Rush family must have struggled. They had to ask themselves what was the point, of his life, of giving birth, of developing love and developing plans, if it were all to be cut so short?

They would have observed a formal mourning. Why don't we do that anymore? It seems like the appropriate response. You would wear your grief so people would know, you would dedicate a period of time to your grief.

They must have wondered about the duration of their pain. There was no place or condition on earth that offered relief but people do promise that time does. They must have had strange thoughts about time like I do.

The house made sense to me then. Four adults, two of them business partners, lived together for years and then the younger couple designed and built their own house on the lot next door. I knew without a doubt the house was the architectural consequence of the second Edwin. A structure of solid masonry and artistic design, beloved by the Rushes, stood for nearly three quarters of a century as evidence of their son. Bricks can talk, some even after they have been scattered, if you can interpret their language. They ultimately proved as good a document as an obituary.

I thought of the hopeful little family that moved into the home, this step into the future for the Rush genealogy, and how death halted their happy momentum. I thought of Edwin, the architect and brief father, his heart calm and open, bringing into reality things that he cared about profoundly but that would not survive.

Then I thought of the Parbels who proliferated autonomous, healthy children and grandchildren there, who also had a namesake son in mortal danger but whose story resolved completely differently. I thought of them filling and cherishing the spaces Edwin Rush created, cherishing them just in time before they were demolished.

This is why I identified with the Rushes, or maybe why they identified with me. Because their buildings were smashed, their name forgotten, their child never reached the age of seven. Their dreams were unfulfilled, like mine. They didn't get to finish their race.

Is the creativity we send into the world only temporary? Is it fragile, capable of destruction by ephemeral conditions or by those ignorant of its value or greedy for their own success? Is it like the biblical scattering of seeds that did not fall on good soil?

Being down to one part-time job with no paid benefits between John and I, was certainly not an appropriate time to indulge my creative writing tendencies.

I found myself spending a great deal of time on it.

I started writing it and some of it became fiction. I described the scene at Amos' funeral, the tension between Edwin and Delia I imagined, the renewal of grief over that earlier loss. I saw Delia so clearly trying to strangle any evidence of emotion for the sake of Edwin and Jessie, and as Edwin turned to look at her, I left them there, unsure of how their lives resolved and unable to finish the scene.

It became a chapter and took its place in a series of chapters proceeding in a strange order that was not chronological. In fact, the chapters seemed to arrange themselves like elements in a landscaped garden, all allowing a different vantage towards the same site. And that focal point was community, the place where we all are joined.

I was developing a new understanding of community. Community encompassed the things that brought us together, as well as the things that separated us. Community was a space that held the products of all of our creativity, and it was an expanse of time that allowed us to honor the contributions of others or destroy them.

In the meantime, I continued to make revelations and connections regarding the Rushes and gush about them to a variety of folks doing local history. That turned out to be a good strategy.

Tom Dilley, a retired attorney, local historian and author, who had devoted himself to the study of our city's cemeteries for decades caught me at the library hurrying to a Grand Rapids Historical Society board meeting one night and excitedly shared an old pamphlet he purchased. It was a Rush architects catalog. I never saw such a full description of their architecture. There were pages of house drawings with narrative and floor plans.

But it wasn't any of those that caused my sharp intake of breath or made me stop in my tracks and call John; it was the publication's only photograph, an image of Edwin and Amos.

It is a photo, succinctly labeled, "The Study", showing both men seated in a homey looking room surrounded by professional and personal accessories.

There are two fishing poles and a wicker basket hanging from a hook in a corner. There is a stovepipe hat on top of a bookcase. The room is crowded with books and journals. The men in their stiff white collars are both intent, Edwin with some publication in his hands. Amos is writing. While its difficult to discern it, you can just make out a cigar stub clenched in Edwin's teeth. There is a drawing table in the foreground that holds a large metal triangle, other drawing tools and floor plans. The wall above the table has framed drawings of homes that could easily be the work of one of the men.

Tom took Rebecca Smith-Hoffman and I on a private cemetery tour one day, a rare treat. I could hardly wait to get to the Rush mausoleum, anxious for any insight. Once there, Tom was able to tell me quite a few details about the art and architecture of the structure. When he talked about the Egyptian revival style, I pressed a point of particular interest.

I asked about the figure over the door. I compared it to a winged disk, a common Egyptian symbol representing rebirth. There are many in the cemetery, one over the door of the Brown pyramid.

I will always remember the response of hesitation that hung for a moment as they studied the stone sculpturing and ultimately could not dismiss it as a simple common symbol. For them the figure seemed too three dimensional, more suggestive of a face. That, of course, is what I wanted them to say.

This allowed me to make a more honest observation, "I think of the child who's here."

Tom began a series of public cemetery tours for the library and historical society that were so popular, the crowds became almost a problem. On a few occasions, he invited me to talk about the Rush mausoleum when we got to it on the tour. This was always fun for me, but never more than the night of the special party for library foundation donors.

The author speaking at a Grand Rapids Public Library Foundation event in August of 2010.

I arrived at Oakhill on a perfect summer evening just as the caterers were spreading white cloths over tables that would hold the food and wine. A party in the cemetery.

I came a little early so I could touch base with Tom. I didn't see him immediately and couldn't get anyone to accept my offer of help so I mingled with the other early arrivers. When I did spot Tom, he introduced me to Paula F., one of Oakhill's main caretakers. She was an instant hero to me. She knew Oakhill, cared about it and cared for it. And she had rare access.

Otherwise we never could have done what we did next.

With little introduction, Tom and Paula invited me to step inside the Brown pyramid. For a moment, in a decidedly Midwestern variation, I was Howard Carter discovering King Tut's tomb.

The Brown pyramid is pretty inside. It has a central Greek column supporting a vaulted ceiling. There are several drawers for bodies, one of which has lost its stone facing, leaving the casket exposed. We could have potentially peeked inside. Tom was especially proud of the expert cut on the pyramid's thick stone doors that resulted in a nearly perfect seal. He insisted that I stand inside with him and observe the pitch black interior with the door closed. I was still holding a plastic cup of Chardonnay.

But it got better.

At one point in the conversation, Tom casually made a comment about the Rush mausoleum's doors being open. I smiled and nodded. I didn't contradict him, but this was a bizarre statement. At that point, I was more familiar with the monument than any living human.

And it even seemed a little cruel since he should understand how seriously I longed for a single glance inside. What secrets about the Rush family might be hinted at only by the interior of this most protected place? What more intimate access could I have to them than to share this sacred space?

There was still time after our exploration of the Brown pyramid and before the start of the tour, so I decided to separate myself from the group and make a quick visit to the Rush tomb. You have to walk down a slightly sloped and curving road. The view is not long. It was a bright, sunny evening and a growing crowd was socializing just a few yards away.

Of all the times I made that approach, I never expected to see what I saw that night, though I'd just been clearly told. It never entered my mind to believe Tom. I didn't trust my own eyes.

The doors were open.

They were open a good three inches, though still behind the padlocked decorative metal gate. Gaping ensued. It was a sublime moment. I'm not sure I can describe it. I'm not sure I need to at this point in this story about my obsession with this mausoleum.

This is what I saw. There were dried leaves lining the edges of the floor just like in Ruth's memory. The stone inside was a quite light color. Since the door opened to the right, we could see the drawers to the left. The handles on the drawers were extraordinary. They were pointy, twisted shapes like young tree branches.

There were no names engraved on the drawers. I would not learn Delia's first name.

The only thing that hinted at personal was the arrangement of the vaults. They ran the length of the sides of the structure. There was space for three drawers stacked one above the other along the left side visible to us. Except the bottom shelf was split in half lengthwise into two shorter vaults. One of these was obviously for six-year-old Edwin, with one to spare for a potential future small body.

Around the time of the party, I was trying to build my description of the death of the child for my writing.

I researched education during the late nineteenth century in general and locally and determined Edwin Harold would have had a year of school.

I explored common causes of childhood mortality during that time period, but then I realized it was possible to do better. I walked to the County Clerk's office from the public library like I'd been instructing patrons of the local history department to do for years. There was a simple one line entry in a log book that served as Edwin Harold's death certificate. It confirmed that he was the son of Edwin and Delia, listed his age as "6 yrs, 5 mos, 28 days" and gave a single word cause of death – peritonitis.

I asked my mom, a retired nurse, about death from peritonitis and then I asked my general practitioner the same when I went for an annual exam. Peritonitis is an infection of the lining of the stomach. It can be caused by an injury (which has always seemed like such a violent possibility to me) or a condition such as a burst appendix.

Through the research and writing, I was getting closer to this death than I would ever have expected.

Two weeks after the cemetery party to the day, another Thursday, I was finishing the death of Eddie in my writing. It was the end of the week for me, the day before a four day Labor Day weekend. It was a split work day. I worked the morning, had a few hours at home and was due back to the library for a three to seven shift.

I was relaxed, alone, writing. I thought I heard the mail arrive, a familiar thump coming from the general direction of the front door. Like you do when you're working on something hard, I allowed this interruption almost without thinking and dashed down the stairs, coming eye to eye with the ghost.

It was small and delicate, appearing more vulnerable to me hanging there than I was to it. It was the white of a hospital sheet, the white of a Christening gown or perhaps a child's burial gown. The wings were the length of the body, straight and elegant. Up between the wings and the head was a kind of fuzzy mantel across the shoulders, royal looking, also pure white.

The most striking characteristic of this specter, however, were the eyes that were so suddenly so close. They were not human eyes, but triangular black spaces, empty of pupils. They did communicate, though, a pathos that struck me deeply, like a very effective cartoon character. I was stopped in my tracks.

Then I rushed and fumbled for the camera and got some imperfect photos. Is evidence of this kind of thing universally impossible? My ghost remained still and tolerated all of this, even when I moved him. Eventually I opened the screen door where the lovely little white moth clung, to fetch the mail, which is what I was doing when he came so powerfully into view.

He touched me and I described him with emotion to at least a couple people that day.

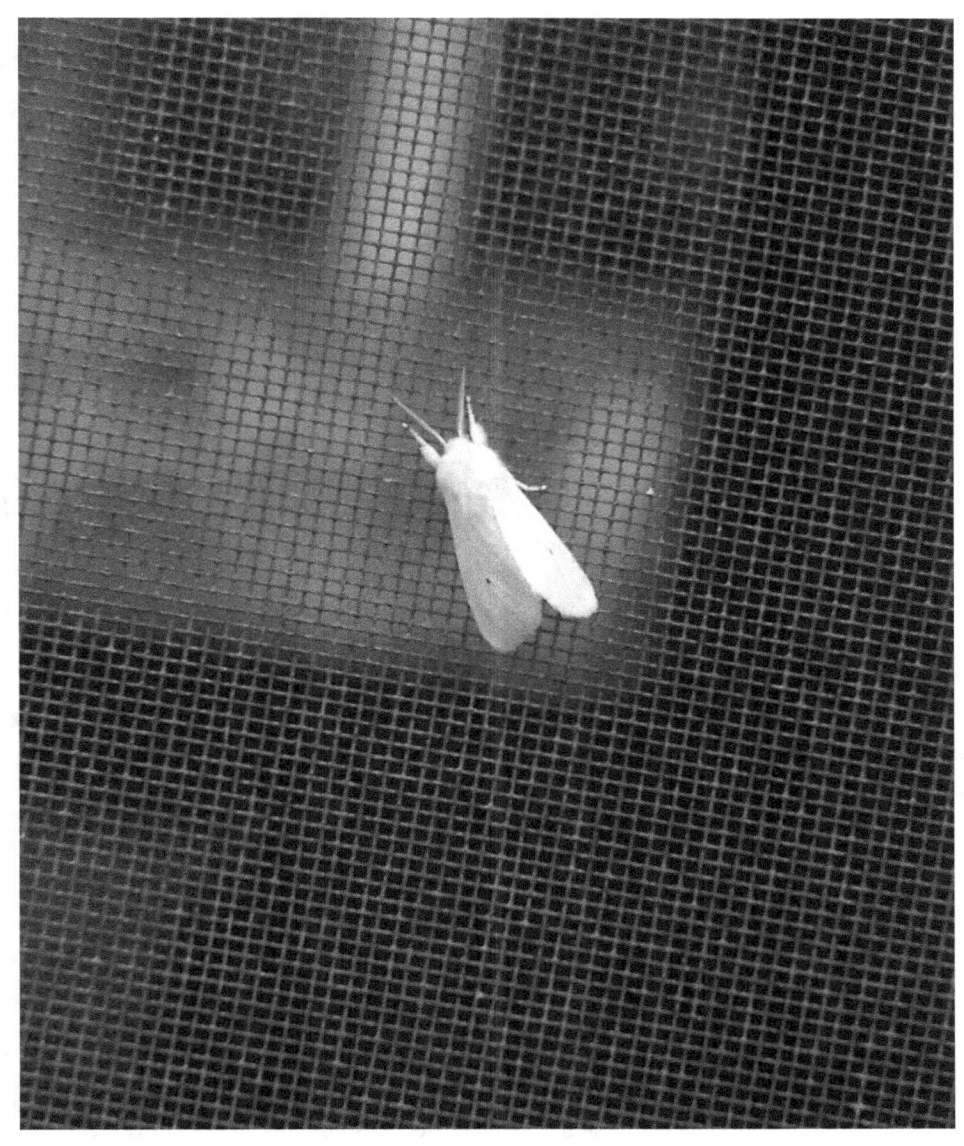

This moth visited the author as she researched and wrote about the death of the Rush child.

The next morning I set the alarm for five, as if it was a work day, and got up to finish the section alone in the predawn, enjoying the novelty of the fact that I could actually return to bed for once if I wanted afterwards. The moth had not moved. He disappeared later that day after I finished writing.

The following Saturday was an anniversary of Edwin Harold's death. I was working at the library. It was a long day and in the afternoon I unexpectedly started to feel sick to my stomach. Later John told me the canned tuna we liked had the same affect on him.

I considered stopping by the cemetery on my way home, just a quick visit by myself, just a simple tribute, but being ill and, frankly, still a touch nervous to do this alone, made me hesitate. So it was a surprise to me when my car followed a different route home and I made the turns into the south half of Oakhill.

It was a cool day with a steady rain. I was the only visitor in the whole cemetery.

I rolled my window down to remove the separation of the car. Raindrops made strange sounds around me. Not wanting to walk at all, I drove to the monument, pulling over to the right of the lane, and parked directly across from the Rush mausoleum.

Sometimes when you do something brave, you get rewarded, there is a sense of triumph, but other times, for some reason, it just doesn't work. You find yourself retreating a little awkwardly, a little defeated. The cemetery had a mood that day. I felt it from the moment I entered.

I didn't want to be afraid. "That's not what this is about," I thought. It seemed juvenile for a grown woman to be spooked, and disrespectful to do it now. I came to extend sympathy. It occurred to me I was just intruding. Perhaps it was me haunting them.

I managed to turn off the car, step out and close the door behind me. I crossed the lane and approached the mausoleum, with a sensation in my gut probably similar to what Ruth felt as a child on her dares.

The doors of the Rush tomb were still open several inches, revealing darkness within. I took a seat on the bench. I probably closed my eyes, tried to focus on an appropriate sentiment, which I achieved briefly, but I couldn't stay. I all but fled, an act that only precipitates panic. Once home I gave in to my nausea, eating very little and going to bed early.

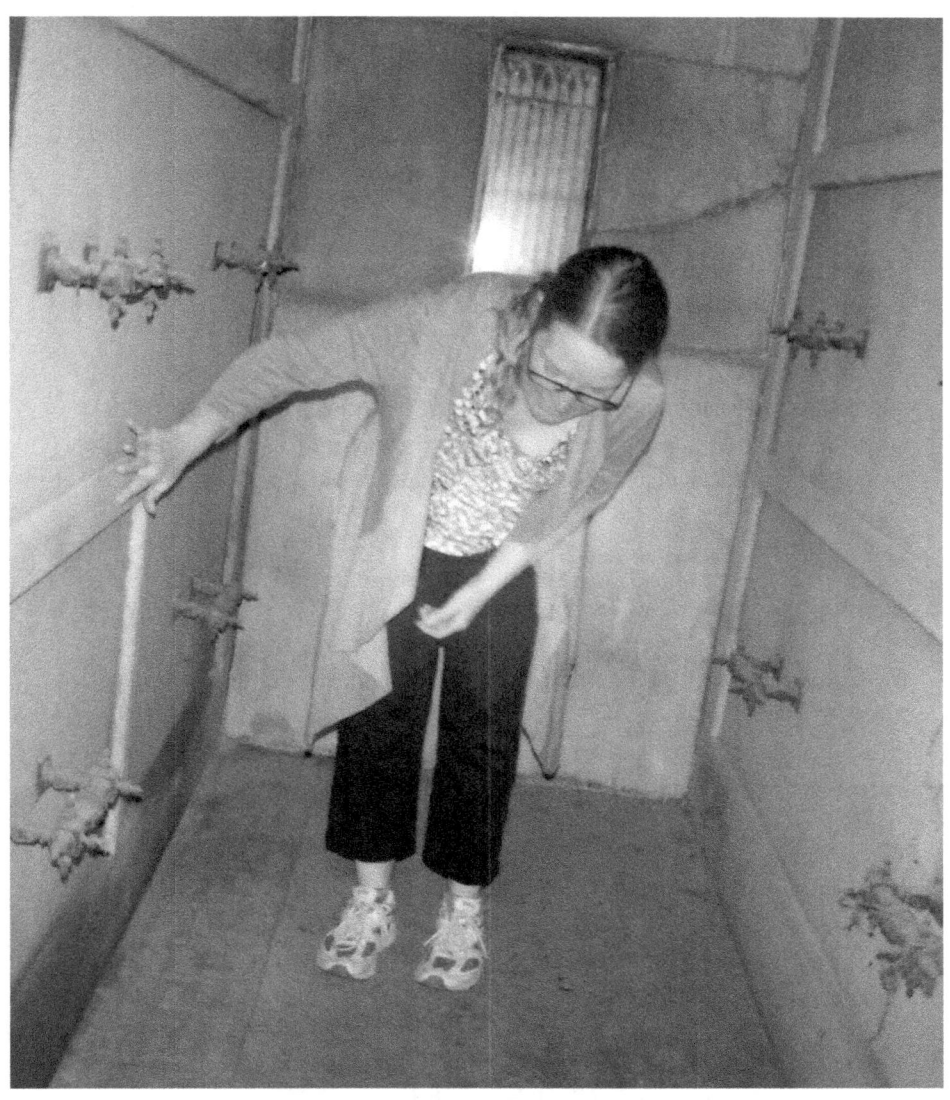

Image inside the Rush mausoleum. The space on the lower left wall of the structure contains two drawers half the length of all the other drawers.

This flurry of intimate moments in the cemetery was nearly over. There was one more rain soaked incident the following Thursday, that split work day. I was home in the middle of the day temporarily. The phone rang and it was Paula Z., who I met the night of the cemetery party. She called and said bluntly that she was inside the Rush mausoleum, giving it a sweep, and asked if I wanted to join her.

The timing was improbably perfect. John and I were there in a little over five minutes.

The day was every bit as wet and gloomy as it had been on my recent solo visit, but the mood was entirely different. Paula had her truck parked close to the mausoleum door, shining her headlights into the interior and sweeping the floor clean. She was cheerful and relaxed. One of those pointy drawer handles got her in the butt and we all had to laugh.

While I had looked into the mausoleum many times by then, at long last, I walked inside.

It was a little difficult to feel dramatic in those circumstances. I tried instead to study every inch of space and memorize it. We took a few photos. Paula wiped off cobwebs and chased the last of the leaves out the door. A lovely Greek key pattern appeared around the edges of the floor, but there were no other surprises.

When we left, Paula was still working inside. As we drove around the back of the mausoleum to leave, she made for a fantastic parting view. I craned my neck to see it as long as I could, the tiny back window framing a human figure silhouetted by light moving around inside. When she finished her work that day, Paula closed the doors of the mausoleum tightly and permanently.

It was a fun spring day in an entirely different Michigan town's cemetery that I found two more members of the Rush family. Besides the two architects and their wives, besides Edwin junior, there were two other children in this family who were forgotten by history.

I found them the day John and I ventured to Lowell, a pretty little nearby town and the place the Rush family lived before they moved to Grand Rapids. Sort of a day trip for us, we explored Main Street and then called our friends, the MacNaughtons, who lived nearby for help locating two things we wanted to find that day - a nice place to get an iced latte and a cemetery.

There was a great place to get a coffee and a decadent scone, but of course it was the cemetery that had the greatest impact that day.

Megan Mac knew right where the main Lowell cemetery was. It was called Oakwood. Faced with the prospect of searching the whole thing, it worked out perfectly that we noticed the Lowell Granite Company located prominently on a Main Street corner. They make headstones.

I suggested we go in and just ask if they knew of a way of navigating Oakwood. There were two people working in the office that day and they treated us as though helping folks searching for gravestones who dropped in unannounced was their principal responsibility. "This is the old section of the cemetery," the woman noted as she pointed out the exact plot on a map.

In the 1920s a group of genealogy minded people walked Kent County's cemeteries and recorded the words on every headstone. Their efforts were converted to index cards kept at the Grand Rapids public library and can be searched by name. I checked them for the name Rush, of course, and discovered the other two.

The Rush family lived in Lowell early enough that Edwin Sr. was a boy there; a boy with a little sister and a baby brother.

Amos and Jessie's other two children never left Lowell. They died of cholera in the summer of 1871. Otto was nearly seven months old when he was lost on July 3, such an infant in the clutches of such a violent disease. One month later to the day, August third, Amos and Jessie's two-year-old daughter succumbed.

I think of hot months, rustic living conditions, multiple children in misery. Edwin was four. Perhaps he was ill as well.

But mostly I think of the echo of these lives and deaths. With the help of the folks from the Lowell Granite Company, we found the marker shared by the youngest Rush children. It is a lovely little tree stone with some nice detail.

The tradition of the marker shaped like a tree is poignant. Typically they are literally truncated to symbolize a life cut short. The Rush monument has the rings delineated and visible from the top, a fern frond near the base, and a smooth spot where the two names and life spans appear: Otto William and Bessie May.

With just her name and dates, Bessie May injected a warm flush of sympathy in me towards her father who disappointed me harshly well into my research, the Amos who gave money to a young mother also named Bessie three decades after losing his only daughter. I remember Caitlin when she was two, what a precious little joy she was. Her personality was evident and she could make us laugh. Caitlin's middle name is Mae.

Many other implications occur. I wonder how the gruesome loss of her two babies shaped Jessie's personality. It might have made her more nervous, more protective. With a child remaining, it could have brought solidarity to the remaining family members. But how profoundly Jessie must have felt her husband's complicated relationship with the adult Bessie, and that Bessie's child.

In hopes of learning more about the Rushes through the people closest to them, I chased their business partners through history. That is how I found Bruce Goff. Goff had a couple attributes of particular value to me. He was quite young when he worked for the Rushes, so he lived longer into the modern age, until 1982 in fact. And he became prominent. Due to both things, he was eventually the subject of recorded interviews. I may be the only one to have read them specifically for any mention of a couple less well known architects from Grand Rapids, Michigan.

Those memories were scarce but they proved important to me. I learned about Goff's boyhood introduction to the Rush firm, instigated by his pushy and probably slightly drunk father.

There was also a note that Goff became interested in Louis Sullivan and Edwin suggested that the apprentice acquaint himself with Sullivan's mausoleums.

Louis Sullivan designed three mausoleums. One of those, located in Chicago's Graceland Cemetery, was for a man from Grand Rapids, Michigan.

As one of the earliest white settlers on the west side of Michigan, Martin Ryerson lived in several places before coming to Grand Rapids where he married and had a child, a namesake son. Martin Sr. eventually became a lumber baron and thus the prestigious Sullivan designed mausoleum where he was laid to rest in 1887 after moving to Chicago. The namesake son spent most of his life in Chicago where he continued the family tradition of wealth as a successful businessman. Martin Jr. also grew prominent in the windy city as an art collector and philanthropist. His name is on the archive at the Art Institute of Chicago. This archive holds the papers of Bruce Goff. Ryerson also remembered his birthplace in his philanthropy. The main branch of the Grand Rapids Public Library, where I worked and did most of my research on the Rush family is named for Martin Ryerson Jr. as he gave the major gift to build it.

It was interesting to see the Ryerson mausoleum. As it happened I had a quite handy view of it when I wanted it. It was Ruth again who was my guide. Her desk was next to mine at work and she had a collection of family photos there, including some of herself posing in front of prominent landmarks on vacation. For years, I walked past the image of her standing with her hands on her hips in front of the Ryerson mausoleum in Graceland Cemetery. When I realized the connection to the Rush family, I just peeked around the cubicle.

Its obvious that Edwin Rush would have been aware of the Ryerson mausoleum, built roughly ten years before the death of Eddie Jr.; and seeing it, it's also obvious it was an inspiration for the Rush monument.

Also among Goff's memoirs was the anecdote about him sneaking into Edwin's office, lured by an open door on a cabinet that was otherwise religiously kept locked. Such opportunities do seem to be universally irresistible.

In the cabinet was a copy of the March 1908 Architectural Record that contained an image and information packed article about Frank Lloyd Wright. I know because GRPL had a copy of the journal in storage and I was able to peruse the same pages that so captivated the young Goff. Wright was just becoming a sensation and Edwin was known to treasure this journal article.

Apparently Goff was not sneaky enough, because Edwin caught him. All that Goff recalled about the confrontation is that Edwin "wasn't angry".

Here again I was confronted with such a minor notation that carried such important emotional weight.

The reference connected me back to my vision of the funeral of Amos and the moment Edwin turned toward Delia as she was trying to hide her grief from those around her and desperately afraid of upsetting her husband. His head was in mid-rotation and she expected a look of impatience from him.

Or in fact I expected that. They were so many years away in a new city where

Edwin resumed a busy and successful career. Delia left no record of activity that I have found. Unlike Amos and Jessie, Edwin and Delia lost their only child. The intensity of that pain, the different lives afterword, must have driven them apart.

I'd been touched by what was lost. But here was evidence that demolition and death were not the whole story. Some of the Rush men's buildings still stood. Of those that are gone forever, through my research I can still see them in their original locations as I travel around my city and they did leave a tangible mark.

Now the death of a six-year-old is an undeniable tragedy. I was certain that it made the Rush family question the very meaning of life, just as I did as I struggled to find a creative outlet that allowed me to connect. But life did undeniably exist in the form of that little boy throughout those years, whether we understand the meaning of that or not, and perhaps there is no life that fails to connect.

After all, his life connected with mine, a complete stranger's, across a century.

Perhaps there is a primal force of love that does not dissipate with the death of the body but remains in some form, in some quiet, forgotten venue, throughout decades, until it meets a prompt and then it can attach and change the life of someone unimagined?

And so as he turns toward his wife on that June morning in my imagination and sees that she is wretched and has begun to jerk with sobs, as the door of Eddie's mausoleum opens to receive the body of Amos, the reaction that I assigned to Edwin matches his wife's. He also has tears in his eyes.

Delia sees a look of tender concern and love on her husband's face.

I decided that after a trip to my mom's house for Thanksgiving one of those first years I was researching the Rush family. There was a bad holiday I'm embarrassed about. All staying at my folks' house, I drank too much one night and lashed out at my brother for being rich and Republican. I was scared to death about money in those days and feeling abandoned.

But we all went back again the next Thanksgiving. I was armed with both a determination to limit my drinking and a small collection of historical documentation. Caitlin's sister, my other niece, Maddie, had a school project on immigration and had to report on her own family's experience. She talked to her mother's Scottish father and I had some great, old photos and documents related to her dad and I's ancestors.

After that holiday, I felt that an unspoken family reparation had taken place. More than that, Maddie's assignment was a reminder of an older, greater connection, something impossible to break, something infinite.

I had a package from Tulsa waiting for me when I got home.

Having been ignored by the historical organizations there, I contacted the genealogy society and those folks will always come through. For them it's personal and your family is just as important as their family, because your family might very well be their family.

They sent me the obituaries for Amos and Jessie, and Edwin and Delia that appeared in the Tulsa newspapers. I can't say that those obits were particularly substantive or had much information that was new for me - except for one small paragraph in Edwin's obit that gave me a gift; more resolution for the Rush family.

The lines read, "Since his retirement, Mr. Rush had devoted much time to the children in his neighborhood. Although he and his wife spent several months each year at their summer home in Michigan, they always were in Tulsa for Halloween to hold open house for neighborhood children. Wednesday afternoon a group of youngsters appeared at the Rush home to present a floral wreath to their friend."

THE STUDY.

The only image found until quite recently of any Rush family member was in a catalog of the architect's house designs that is in the private collection of author and historian, Thomas R. Dilley.

Source Notes

This chapter takes the form of memoir, like chapters two, four and six. Since it describes my local history research, sources are detailed in the narrative.

The photograph of the Rush men is in the following publication:

Rush's Annual. (Grand Rapids: E.A. Rush & Company, Publishers, n.d.) Private collection of Thomas R. Dilley

This obituary figures prominently in the Rush family story and is referenced in this chapter:

"Arthur Rush, 81, Succumbs." Tulsa Daily World. October 21, 1948.

All author photos except image on page 150.

Keeping the Door Open

Edwin Rush junior gives me hope.

It's ironic. He died at six years old with nearly all of his potential unrealized. Of the dreams that his parents even had time to develop for him, nearly all of those were stifled. He was an only child and ended a family line. He left almost no documentation of his life and his family left very little of theirs.

And yet, here we are talking about him.

A stranger who happened along over a hundred years after he departed was able to connect with him, to explore the details and the implications of his life and his loss, to understand at least a little how he affected the people and the world around him, to care.

And I absolutely became a partner in the connection. I believe my concern was specifically rewarded in the form of a few sentences about a Halloween party and a floral wreath that were included in an otherwise brief and unremarkable obituary.

It's been over ten years since Caitlin and I happened upon the Rush mausoleum. She is now an inner-city grade school teacher. She is brave and good and really fun. She seems destined to do hard work with kids that need a great deal. She lives in a different state in a big midwestern city that fascinates me. I'm sure I would find its story both familiar and entirely unique. John and I visited her there. While she was working, we explored a huge, thrilling, Victorian cemetery and happened, without any introduction, across a simply amazing mausoleum with a few secrets.

I am no longer at the Grand Rapids Public Library. There is a truly awesome archivist in charge of the local history department there. Recently I started a fulltime job with benefits as an archivist for the Dominican Sisters of Grand Rapids, a group of educated women who have dedicated their lives to social justice. They inspire me deeply. This is basically my dream job. I am so fortunate.

In between working at the public library and coming to work for the Sisters, I had a stint as the sole archivist for two local institutions of higher learning. I particularly loved working with students. Sometimes I only met them briefly to give them advice for research projects; but I also got a student assistant every semester and I even created and taught a 300 level, sixteen-week public history class. Some of those students have now gone into the field. I became the Edwin who reacted to the young Bruce Goff steeling a glimpse of his Architectural Journal. These are special connections for me.

It was while I was still in my thirties one day in an office down some halls and around some corners in a sprawling medical complex in Grand Rapids when a specialist told John and I that we could never have children naturally, related the shocking cost of invitro fertilization. I remember the news specifically making me feel old, and old was the quality of having permanently missed out on opportunities that did exist for me when I was younger. For some reason I still own a white onesie with nursery rhyme characters on it that I received when we were trying. It's in the bottom of my underwear drawer.

Mystically, perhaps only falsely, something tangible like that can give the impression of access to possibility. Like a mausoleum door.

I've survived cancer. Since recovery, I exceeded my previous distance record for running - by one mile. I haven't lost that opportunity. I'm still not very fast and I still don't care. During my years of cancer treatment, my oncologist had an office in the Lemmen-Holton building and I enjoyed an unprecedented view of the corner of Coit and Hastings Street where the Rush home sat one hundred years earlier. There is still neighborhood-changing development taking place in that corridor and throughout my city. Until recently, I thought we'd learned the value of historic preservation and the mistake of trying to destroy history.

Of course, when I started this journey, I also thought we had evolved beyond segregation and largely even racism. I had a lot to learn. Some of that has been made clear by a family I never met who all died before I was born, or rather, by my attempt to understand how that family and I fit into the same city's development. The past tends to disappear from view, it fades and breaks into puzzle pieces we have to put back together; but seeking out Rush family and architecture increased that view to an exciting new depth for me.

I saw relationships between buildings and people, between people from different time periods, between people and their communities, between the unique and broader historical trends. I often thought my puzzle was like one of those pictures you have to stare at just right and suddenly a three-dimensional image appears. I gained a better understanding of how Grand Rapids and, by extension, other cities evolved.

Industrialization at the end of the nineteenth century sent people streaming into urban areas. Populations doubled and tripled and kept growing. Architecture and infrastructure boomed, as did opportunity for some. The Rush family was at the center of all of that.

It happened again when the family moved to Tulsa. The Rushes helped construct American cities. Those cities endured but not without problems. Tulsa's race massacre is a powerful example.

I came to realize that cities concentrated people into smaller areas, an ever increasing variety of people, and often that did not go well. There is just as much challenge as possibility in such a dynamic.

It seemed as though, ironically, one of the methods people negotiated their way in communal spaces was by pretending the others weren't there. We continue to do that. When they walk past us on the sidewalk, we turn away and deepen our conversation with the ones we do recognize. We put up fences and walls to keep each other out, always trying to increase our own acreage and dispose of our waste on someone else's portion.

We also like to pretend that we are the first ones here.

After the early expansion, there were bust years as well for the American city. Infrastructure lagged, buildings aged, people moved out. This decay still threatens and weakens us.

The impact of the mid-century was a revelation to me since I did not grow up in a city and previously had no interest in such modern history. This half way point between the Rush's time and mine impressed me as a collision, not just of bricks and men but of the present and the past. Competing interests and needs became even harder to separate.

As for bricks, we started to pull down the previous generation's urban architecture. As for men trying to get along in the same space, it is impossible to overestimate how central our failure to do this figures into the fate of the midwestern city. All those lurid tales of riots and violence, all those graphic images of bulldozers maiming beautiful buildings, made me think something crested and crashed. A great deal of energy collapsed, with reverberations repeating the pattern.

In my day, there are signs of improvement. I moved to Grand Rapids because I believed it was flourishing. There was a symphony and a zoo and fun restaurants. I can enjoy such things as bike lanes and a beer industry, but I still live in a segregated city. I still live in an area where the architecture and streetscapes of the artists and planners who came before us are leveled too hastily to line the pockets of too few.

I now see those lost buildings when I move around the city. Staring at and comparing contemporary photos and maps will give you something like the perspective of much older people who knew the former landscape firsthand.

I see demolished buildings and dead people, like Delia Rush at Oakhill, but I also see people who haven't been born yet.

There was a woman at a market that kept showing up in my imagination while I was working on this manuscript.

I had a hazy picture of her. She was in Grand Rapids in the near future. It was a sunny summer day and she wore light clothing. The market featured a variety of both necessary and appealing offerings to help her with her appetite (plump tomatoes featured prominently), her health, her home life and even her social life.

For me, there is an obvious link between the past and the future. The past determines so much about the future and that is why it is so important to hang onto our view of it while we move forward. The woman at the market existed to help me manifest my hopes for the future in my imagination.

The woman's community is different from mine partly because our view of community has changed in her time. I imagine a better manifestation of community for her. We do not all have to make such an expensive investment in material culture, for example. We become better at recognizing our common needs and cooperating to fulfill them.

She and the market are near Oakhill Cemetery and the cemetery is returned to an excellent state of maintenance. More than that, it has exceeded the role it ever played before as a cultural center and community asset.

The smaller, older homes nearby have gained preference over the huge, generic, suburban sprawl housing developments of my day. People have embraced minimalism and a smaller footprint on the environment. Smarter energy policies have resulted from advances in science and technology. More people want good construction and established neighborhoods.

The early commercial buildings near her home have been put to adapted reuse. Historic preservation and city planning are valued and routinely taken into consideration together. This is a sustainable practice and makes economic sense. There are more careers in historic preservation and applied history in general.

Work life has been transformed in her day. There is a more fluid relationship between skills and/or interests and the demand for them. No one has to occupy an uncomfortable remote office space for forty hours a week or trade time for money. People's basic human needs are met despite their contribution to the commercial economy. This is part of a larger shift that includes things as varied as the energy revolution, the disillusionment with materialism and a broader tendency to pursue social justice instead of personal gain.

There is much greater recognition of our common humanity including more advanced anti-racism. Ironically, I learned so much about racism from a late nineteenth century father and son architect. I discovered the harm it caused to their buildings and the pain it caused to the people who inhabit those buildings and this city we all share. I, like many, want a future where opportunity is more equal, and where we are all recognized as vital parts of the story.

I still have a lot to learn. I'm still so naïve. Can we get to this future?

I've seen some powerful evidence lately that we have way, way farther to go than I ever realized, and I've seen some beautiful glimpses of hope. There is so much exhausting work to do. And I've seen some good people breaking that work into jobs, signing up for them and putting in their time and talent to complete them.

I'm sure the market in my vision symbolizes the archetypal community space. It is the place where we confront each other. Despite white flight and urban sprawl and all our considerable powers of exclusion, our focus on not seeing each other, our over-policing and protectionism; ultimately it is impossible to escape community. We must negotiate every relationship in our lives, including the people we are closest to in the world and the people who just moved in across the street who look and act in ways that make us nervous.

Open Mausoleum Door

Throughout my interest in history, I've wondered how I would respond in certain situations and I've tried to accept my responsibility to the past and all the people who have paved my relatively comfortable way. But doing the right thing as a citizen of a community is complicated. Or is it?

We have made it so far as a People but are we getting closer or further away from the ideals of community? I haven't been able to decide conclusively one way or another. Are we doing this better in cities than in rural America, because we are less able to avoid it?

We do persist in connecting by making our contributions: books, buildings, babies; and sending them out into the world and into the future.

And sometimes the future knows exactly what to do with them. Sometimes the future does actually resolve the past.

In the fullness of time, the Universe never forgets a single contribution.

We must continue to leave the door open to possibility.

Acknowledgements

This book has been in process for some time, during which many people contributed to its improvement whether significantly or simply by answering a reference question in passing. At some point, I realized this project was teaching me about the concept of community, and it is a community that I relied on to accomplish what I have.

I would like to start by thanking Caitlin, who gave me a Christmas present that turned into one of the most enduring and fascinating projects I have ever pursued. Thanks also to her sister, her parents and my parents for their support of me. Thank you to my husband, John, for his willingness to live with, accommodate, and assist with my obsession.

I am particularly indebted to those who gave me interviews and allowed me to use their precious family memories to explore my interests and record my observations. Those people include the late Rosemary Parbel Kilmartin, the late John Logie, and Ruth VanStee.

Many members of Grand Rapids' local history community helped me over the years. I am grateful to them for the work they do and their eagerness to share it. Outstanding among them were Rebecca Smith Hoffman and Thomas R. Dilley, who always responded to my requests of them with their time, effort, promptness, and generosity.

Photographs added a great deal to my manuscript. Thank you to Julie Tabberer at the Grand Rapids Public Library, Andrea Melvin at the Grand Rapids Public Museum, the Art Institute of Chicago, Anne Azkoul (daughter of Rosemary Parbel Kilmartin), Thomas R. Dilley, and Ruth Van Stee.

I am deeply thankful for the existence of the Grand Rapids History Center at the Grand Rapids Public Library. All those responsible for this rich, fascinating, and important collection are local heroes.

Valuable editing was given by Aquinas College interns, Rose Treutle and Jonah Chickering. Thank you also to a small host of beta readers and other friends who listened to me and discussed this project with me, some rather extensively. Special thanks are due to five people who gave the manuscript its final read, sharing their expertise and prioritizing my request despite their own complicated schedules: Gina Bivens, Matthew Daley, Thomas R. Dilley, Rebecca Smith Hoffman and Julie Tabberer.

Thank you to talented friend, Roger MacNaughton, who wrote a song based on my manuscript.

Thank you to Dionne Wetzel who took a bunch of text and photos and made them into a book, including designing the book cover.

Finally, thank you to Schuler Books: first, just for being there with books and magazines and lattes and warm soup and a fireplace all these years (you are one of my favorite places on Earth) and more relevantly for your Espresso Book Machine and Chapbook Press that allow this outlet for local authors.

Open Mausoleum Door

Open Mausoleum Door